NORTH SEA FERRIES

Ships of the Night

by

Barry Mitchell

HUTTON PRESS

1991

Published by the Hutton Press Ltd.,
130 Canada Drive, Cherry Burton,
Beverley, North Humberside HU17 7SB

Typeset and printed by
Image Colourprint Ltd.
Anlaby, Hull.

ISBN 1 872167 30 6

Contents

Acknowledgements

I am indebted to all North Sea Ferries' staff both ashore and at sea who have kindly contributed to this publication. It would be impossible to individually name each and every person who, over my long association with the Company, have provided a wealth of information. To all of them I wish to express my sincere thanks.

My gratitude reaches out to the senior management for their unfailing co-operation to my requests for access to their ships, archive materials and photographic files. Here a special 'thank you' must go to co-ordinator Mr. Tony Farrell for his perpetual support, advice and assistance. Without backing of this nature there would have been no book.

Away from the company I record many thanks to my wife Mollie and daughter Suzanne for their help and patience whilst I have been preoccupied with the project.

Finally I express my sincere appreciation to the enthusiastic group of photographers who have provided such a wealth of material for this book. My only regret is that there is not sufficient space to print all the excellent camerawork offered.

Barry Mitchell,
Bridlington,
October 1991.

Photographs

North Sea Ferries Collection:- Herbert Ballard, Hull. Donald Innes, Hessle. Skyfotos, New Romney, Kent. Nic B. Morellis. Luchfoto, Bart Hofmeester. P.A. Kroehnert, Bremerhaven. Aero Camera, Rotterdam. Frans L. Reijnders. Seebeckwerft AG. N K K Corporation.
Michael E. Drewery. Jim Draper. Mike Barnard. Jan Meyer. Hull Daily Mail. The News, Portsmouth. Govan Shipbuilders. Studio Acht. L. Davison. Ministry of Defence. Hull City Council. Luchtfotografie Henderyckx-Izegem. Wil Barkmeijer.

Graphics

Mike Barnard, Bridlington.

About the Author

Barry Mitchell was born and educated in West Yorkshire. He served as a short term regular in the Royal Air Force and spent three years as a Radar Operator on the Yorkshire Coast.

Having stage by stage walked the paths and tracks along the coastline Barry Mitchell gathered sufficient knowledge of the area to write his first book *Exploring the Yorkshire Coast*.

Now long settled in the seaside town of Bridlington he has written several magazine articles chiefly of a nautical nature. It was however, his book *Ro-Ro to Finland* that won him much acclaim in the maritime world. Regarded as the most complete work covering a ro-ro operation this Hutton Press title follows the voyage of a modern freighter around Scandinavia.

Apart from his interest in the sea and ships, the author also enjoys rambling amidst the fells and mountains of the Yorkshire Dales and English Lake District. Keen on boating he takes every opportunity to spend leisure time on Britain's inland waterways.

Over a number of years Barry Mitchell has made sea voyages to all of the Scandinavian countries, likewise he has regularly crossed to the countries of the near continent via North Sea Ferries - a situation leading to *Superferries*, his first title about the company, and culminating in this book.

Married with one daughter the author appropriately lives within sight and sound of the North Sea.

North Sea Ferries - Ships of the Night

'North Sea Ferries - Ships of the Night' is my second book covering this internationally renowned ferry operation. In choosing a title for this work I looked for the most suited Precis for the vehicular function of the company's operation - nightly indeed, with more than 26 years of continuous North Sea crossings behind them, 'Ships of the Night' the N.S.F. vessels most certainly are!

While retaining some of the material from its predecessor, *Superferries*, this volume is aimed to fulfil requests for an extended photographic vista. Whole new collections of past and present illustrations have been made available. Here one will find the new presentation format has provided the opportunity to do justice to this material together with previous photographs and graphics.

In order to create further space for illustrated matter earlier text content has been condensed. However, the North Sea Ferries' story is still as complete and here readers will probably recognise the retention of several passages which are vital in accurately describing the company's history and operational mode.

I sincerely hope that the reader will derive some of the enjoyment and illumination from this publication that I have experienced in its preparation.

Barry Mitchell.

Norland prepares to sail on N.S.F.'s 6pm departure for Rotterdam. The self and same overnight schedules have been continually maintained since the company's 1965 beginnings. This 1975 winter scene at Hull epitomizes 'North Sea Ferries - Ships of the Night'.

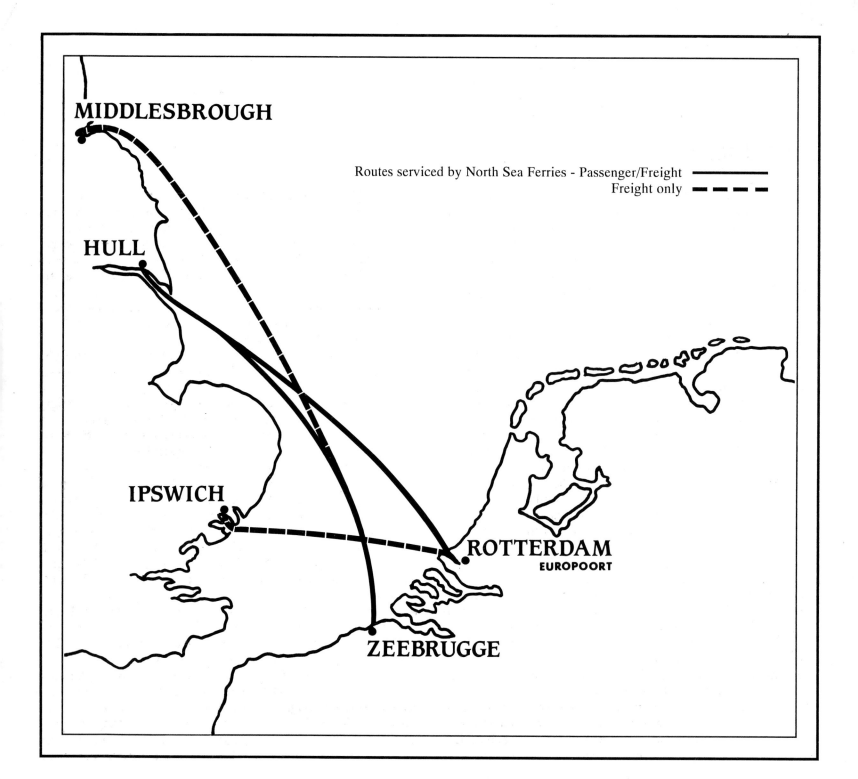

MIDDLESBROUGH

HULL

IPSWICH

ROTTERDAM
EUROPOORT

ZEEBRUGGE

Routes serviced by North Sea Ferries - Passenger/Freight
Freight only

Introduction

For more than a quarter century North Sea Ferries' ships have crossed the North Sea nightly - if one discounts the respite of earlier New Year and Christmas Days, the claim can be 'every single night of each year'. Conceived on foresight of a more integrally linked Europe, North Sea Ferries was a successful venture from its first days of operation, subsequently commencing growth, demand/ supply related, at a pace that has been maintained to the very present day.

This all began in the early 1960s when Mr. Ian Churcher, a leading figure in European transport circles, predicted coming trends in continental travel and the advent of wheeled freight operations. Throughout Western Europe this was a period of rapid growth both in the family car population and the newfound pursuit of holidays abroad. Additionally motorways and autobahns were steadily spreading tendrils that ultimately would link major ports with principal industrial centres on both sides of the North Sea. Moreover, with the awakening to the economic advantages of containerization and unit loads, road transport was rapidly gaining favour over rail freight systems. Mr. Churcher saw an imminent desire for through traffic from the Midlands, North of England and Scotland to the vast network of continental trunk roads and vice-versa. His enthusiasm for purpose built ferries to fulfil this approaching need led to a consortium of six European interests (2 British 2 German 2 Dutch) investing in the building of two 4,000 gross ton drive-on drive-off ships. They were to sail overnight Hull/ Rotterdam (Europoort) in each direction six days a week under the appropriate label of North Sea Ferries. While designed to accommodate 249 passengers the ferries were also to carry a mix of unitized freight, lorries of unlimited length and private cars of either holiday travellers or business people.

Subsequently, December 17th 1965 saw the maiden voyage of m.v. *Norwave* and the inauguration of the highly successful N.S.F. operation. Special passenger terminals had been constructed both at Hull's King George Dock and Beneluxhaven, a new formed harbour within Rotterdam's Europoort complex. Together with appropriate passenger facilities link span ramps provided an unimpeded drive-on drive-off amenity for all vehicular traffic at both terminals.

Although initially much criticized by pundits from the conventional shipping world the route had already gained a sizable share of North Sea freight traffic and established new horizons for passenger trade when, in March 1966, *Norwave*'s sister ship *Norwind* entered service. Then able to cover the intended daily 'each direction' sailing commitment, these 'first generation' vessels steadily built up a reputation of versatility and reliability. This situation soon led to seven day week sailings and has undoubtedly proved to be a fundamental of the N.S.F. success story.

Inevitably the mid 1970's saw the birth of the 'second generation' ships. Such had the popularity of the Hull/Rotterdam service grown that *Norwave* and *Norwind* had neither the capacity to carry the numbers of seasonal travellers or the deluge of year-round freight available for the route. Indeed, in respect of the latter a succession of chartered ro-ro freighters together with two lift-on lift-off vessels had been used to augment capacity on the service.

Norland was the first of the new generation to arrive. At almost 13,000 gross tons she was at that time the largest ferry of her kind in the world and in every aspect represented a vast expansion to the 'first generation' ships. *Norland* had been delivered from the Bremerhaven yards of A.G. Weser, birthplace of the earlier ships and the location of where her sister ship *Norstar* was well on the way to completion. Originally labelled as 'jumbo' ferries these 1243 passenger capacity ships took over the, by then prestigious, Hull/Rotterdam service.

Already a N.S.F. freight only service had been established between Hull and the Belgian port of Zeebrugge. Consequently as the displaced *Norwave* and *Norwind* became available a N.S.F. passenger link with Zeebrugge was pioneered.

At Hull much shore development had been carried out by the then British Transport Docks Board in order to accommodate the larger ships and the new Belgian service. A new car terminal was officially opened by H.R.H. Princess Margaret in October 1974 appropriately being named 'The Princess Margaret Terminal'. Equally a large capacity terminal was constructed at the N.S.F. Rotterdam base together with passenger facilities at Prins Filipdok, Zeebrugge.

In this format N.S.F.'s second epoch began. It was to be a period of some thirteen years marked by a progression of significant events. Not least of these happenings was the departure of Ian Churcher who in June 1975 was appointed Executive Chairman with P & O Ferries. Mr. Churcher was ultimately awarded an O.B.E. for his services to the shipping industry. His position at the helm of N.S.F. was filled by Mr. Jaap Feringa, formerly manager with Royal Interocean Lines. It was during Mr. Feringa's $3\frac{1}{2}$ year term of office at the company's Rotterdam headquarters that the N.S.F. Ipswich/Rotterdam freight-only service was opened. Initially operated with charter ships the route is now covered on a two crossings in each direction per day basis by the N.S.F. sister ships *Norsky* and *Norcape*.

North Sea Ferries' next Managing Director, Mr. Graeme Dunlop, took office on February 1st 1979 having previously held a similar post with the Arabian Peninsular Container Line. During the ensuing years Mr. Dunlop steered N.S.F. through some of the most prominent stages in its brief history. In 1981 N.S.F. became a joint venture between the P & O Group and the Royal Nedlloyd Group of the Netherlands each company holding 50% share in the operation owning *Norwave/Norland* and *Norwind/ Norstar* respectively.

Subsequently plans were drawn up to build two superferries with a view to replacing the ageing 'first generation' vessels. However the plans were shelved until 1985 when orders were eventually given to shipyards in Britain and Japan to proceed with simultaneous construction. It was during the interim period (April 1982) that *Norland* was requisitioned by the Ministry of Defence to sail to the South Atlantic as a troop ship. This resulted in a 12 month period of absence of a principal company unit and ultimately a most anxious time for the owners, the crew and their families. Following an extensive refit *Norland* was reunited with sister *Norstar* on the Hull/ Rotterdam service in the Spring of 1983 again subscribing to the popularity of the route.

In June 1985 a further logistical problem hit the N.S.F. management when *Norland* was holed shortly after leaving Rotterdam. Though the ship was towed safely back to port the ingress of water caused extensive engine room damage, repairs to which took $10\frac{1}{2}$ weeks. But by now the two year building schedule for the two 31,500 gross ton 'third generation' superferries was well under way. September 9th 1986 saw the launching of the P & O sponsored *Norsea* by Queen Elizabeth the Queen Mother at the Govan yards of British Shipbuilders. Just twelve days earlier her sister ship *Norsun*, the Nedlloyd 'third generation' contribution, had slipped down the ways without ceremony halfway across the world at the Nippon Kokan yards at Yokohama. *Norsea* was the largest passenger vessel to be built in Britain since Q.E.2 in 1967 and one of the most sophisticated ships from any British yard in recent years.

At Hull an entirely new £5 million terminal system, including a centralised terminal building (constructed by Associated British Ports exclusively for N.S.F.), was well on its way to completion when on December 17th 1986 the company celebrated its 21st anniversary. But with the impending spring arrival of the 'third generation' ships the focus was very much on the future. At the beginning of 1987 the pace related to this event gathered momentum not least in the form of a systematic introduction of a new two-tone blue livery and company logo.

Added to the progression at that time was the confirmation of plans to lengthen *Norland* and *Norstar*. Speculation of this undertaking had been mounting for more than six months. Results of extensive surveys had declared the feasibility of stretching the 'second generation' sisterships by slicing them open and inserting a 20.25 metre mid-section. The operation was to be carried out over a period of seven weeks at the Bremerhaven shipyard where the sisters were built in 1974. On completion *Norland* and *Norstar* were to enter the Hull/Zeebrugge service in July 1987 as new-look superferries with rearranged passenger accommodation and greatly increased freight capacity.

Meanwhile the long awaited *Norsea* and *Norsun* arrived on service on May 8th and 12th respectively. Boasting space and luxuries not experienced on earlier North Sea services, the two 'superferries' won immediate approval from the ever-increasing numbers of people travelling with the company. At Hull the new terminal complex was by now fully operational - it was officially named and opened by H.R.H. Princess Margaret on July 15th, 1987.

By this time a change in respect of the head of the company had taken place. Mr. Dunlop had been relocated as Managing Director of P & O European Ferries and his position had been filled by Mr. Remi Speld of the Royal Nedlloyd Group. Mr. Speld stayed with N.S.F. up to the summer of 1990 (handing over the helm to Mr. Russ Peters of P & O). Though his term at the Rotterdam headquarters had been relatively brief the growth of business during this period had been meteoric. The "new look" operation had attracted a virtual 100% increase in passenger traffic in the space between the company's 21st birthday and its Silver Jubilee in 1990. Moreover one-million passengers had been carried during the Jubilee year - this goal being an early objective of Mr. Churcher's. But sadly the founder and former head of the company had died two years prior to its realisation. With the introduction of a new freight-only ro-ro service operating between Middlesbrough and Zeebrugge in 1988, a back-up ro-ro vessel on the Hull/Rotterdam route in 1989 and an additional berth constructed in 1990 to service the Ipswich/Rotterdam operation, the freight side of the business had been equally expansive.

When on December 17th, 1990 *Norsun* departed on the Hull/ Rotterdam crossing she was carrying 300 guests of the company only. This special 'Silver Jubilee' cruise was a celebration of what N.S.F. advertise as '25 years of excellence'. It was indeed a memorable occasion for as the big ship, festooned in streamers, hauled into the winter night the reflection was on the past - what a momentous era had unfolded since *Norwave* had pioneered the very same route and schedule exactly a quarter of a century earlier.

NORTH SEA FERRIES SHIPS AND SERVICES

Hull/Rotterdam	*Norsea/Norsun*	each of 31,598 grt.
	Norcove	
	(Chartered Ship,	
	Freight Only	3,933 grt.
Hull/Zeebrugge	*Norland/Norstar*	each of 26,919 grt.
Ipswich/Rotterdam	*Norsky/ Norcape*	each of 6,310 grt.
Middlesbrough/Zeebrugge	*Norking/Norqueen*	each of 6,850 grt.
	(Chartered Ships)	

Only over a space of three hours were the first three generations of N.S.F. ships represented in line together. N.S.F. Captain Jan Meyer seized the opportunity of this unique photograph at Hull 8th May, 1987. From the left, *Norsea, Norland* and *Norwind.*

Norwave, first commanded by Captain Cyril Reynolds, on one of her early Hull/Rotterdam crossings. In $21\frac{1}{2}$ years continuous service *Norwave* and her sistership *Norwind* each covered $1\frac{1}{2}$ million nautical miles in over 7,000 crossings.
(N.S.F. Collection).

1. In the Beginning - Norwave/Norwind

Norwave and *Norwind* were built at the yards of A.G. Weser, Bremerhaven, W. Germany entering service 17th December 1965 and 22nd March 1966 respectively. On launching the N.S.F. operation and the Hull/Rotterdam service, they continued on the route until June 1974 and December 1974 when the 'second generation' sisters *Norland* and *Norstar* respectively entered service. From these dates *Norwave* and *Norwind* spent a further 13 years operating the N.S.F. Hull/Zeebrugge service. Apart from short periods set aside for statutory surveys, maintenance and repairs, both vessels crossed the North Sea almost every night for a marathon period of $21\frac{1}{2}$ years.

These 'first generation' sisters were not initially renowned for their good looks, considering the sheer and rake of conventional ships of the day. In marked contrast they displayed cliff-like black and white hull walls that lifted perpendicular from the water. A blunt rounded bow opened in the manner of a whale's mouth while their white stepped superstructure was crowned with a three-cornered bridgehouse. Not least an athwartships crossmember linked two side-by-side exhaust uptakes the likes of which had not been seen on the Humber before. In all respects they could have claimed to have been 'ahead of their time', for many of these 'new' innovations represented the shape of things to come.

Initially the Hull/Rotterdam service was operated six nights a week. However through demand this frequency was increased to seven when Saturday night sailings were introduced in 1967. Naturally there were occasions when bad weather and unforeseen circumstances delayed these ships but, registered against the enormous number of completed scheduled crossings, they can be dismissed as negligible. The greatest period of absence was that of *Norwave* late 1983 having suffered an engine room fire while in the Humber outward bound for Zeebrugge. Her passengers were taken ashore at Immingham and ultimately she was towed to Amsterdam where repairs took six weeks. During this period *Norwind* fulfilled the passenger commitment on the Belgian run unaided.

Norwave and *Norwind* always proved popular with passengers who enjoyed a 'small ship' atmosphere and many will recall convivial evenings in the cosy setting of the after end 'Snug Bar'. Regardless, as time advanced not only did their capacity of 249 passengers become inadequate to fulfil demand but lack of the facilities expected by travellers two decades-on became apparent. Amongst the ever increasing travelling population were elderly, and disabled passengers. Here the absence of internal passenger lifts to link public rooms with the main cabin space on 'G' deck became a regular irritation. Similarly disadvantageous was their restricted cargo capacity, a situation that required a back-up of chartered ro-ro freighters to cover shipper's demands on the popular Belgian circuit.

Indeed the Hull/Zeebrugge service offered wide scope for expansion, yet, while continuing to operate the 'first generation' vessels, the company were unable to exploit its full potential. Nevertheless, their compactness continued to lend a distinct air of friendliness, both having the enviable reputation of being 'happy ships'. This together with a long proven mechanical reliability and safety record led one to believe that they would cross the North Sea indefinitely.

However, *Norwave* and *Norwind*, pioneers of both N.S.F.'s freight/passenger routes, made their final overnight crossings for the company on 30th June and 5th July 1987 respectively. They had been sold to the Greek Ventouris Line for their Patras/Corfu/Bari service. Within two days of completing her last voyage for N.S.F. *Norwave* sailed out of Zeebrugge for the Mediterranean as *Italia Express*. *Norwind* (now named *Grecia Express*) made the short canal journey to Brugges pending collection by her new owners in the late Summer of 1987.

Finalising *Norwave*'s story was disturbing news received from Greece in Spring 1988. While berthed by the stern awaiting repairs at Drapetzona shipyard near Piraeus on 24th March *Italia Express* sank under strange circumstances in almost 30 metres of water. An explosion was heard by a watchman and within 20 minutes the faithful old ship was gone. There were no casualties.

It is understood that to-date *Grecia Express* (ex. *Norwind*) continues to ply Greek waters.

Technical Data

	M.V. *Norwave*	M.V. *Norwind*
Building Yard	A.G. Weser, Bremerhaven, W. Germany	
Completed	December 1965	March 1966
Port of Registry	Hull	Rotterdam
Services		
Hull/Rotterdam	17th December 1965 to June 1974	22nd March 1966 to December 1974
Hull/Zeebrugge	June 1974 to 30th June 1987	December 1974 to 5th July 1987
Gross Tonnage	4,000	4,000
Deadweight Tonnage	1,953	1,953
Displacement Tonnage	5,305	5,305
Length	108.8m (357 feet)	108.8m (357 feet)
Breadth	18.8m (61 feet)	18.8m (61 feet)
Draught	5.11m (17 feet)	5.11m (17 feet)
Passengers	249	249
Cargo	47 x 12m units + 70 cars or any mix	
Engines	2 Smit Bolnes V314D totalling 5,200 h.p.	
Service Speed	16 knots	16 knots
Stabilisers	Tranquilduct	Tranquilduct
Crew	50	50
Flag	British	Dutch
New Owners	Ventouris Group, Greece.	
Renamed	*Italia Express* (Reported sunk Drapetzona, Greece, 24th March, 1988).	*Grecia Express*

After-end profile of *Norwave* as she nears completion at the Bremerhaven shipyard of WG Weser in December 1965. Newly launched sister ship *Norwind* lies alongside.
(N.S.F. Collection).

One of *Norwind*'s Smit-Bolnes main engines being lowered through the carcase of the new ship's hull. 1965.
(N.S.F. Collection).

Above: Varied traffic drives aboard *Norwind* at Europoort in the late 1960's. The berth and terminal used by the 'first generation' ships was adapted for the company's Ipswich/ Rotterdam freight only service in 1977. A second freight-only berth was opened nearby in December 1990. (N.S.F. Collection).

Right: Norwave at Prins Filipsdock, Zeebrugge. The 'first generation' ships used this terminal from 1974 until 1985 when the present-day terminal opened at the outer harbour.

The 'first generation' ships after-end 'Snug Bar' was always a popular rendezvous. Seasoned travellers with N.S.F. will recall many convivial evenings spent in its cosy atmosphere.
(N.S.F. Collection).

This rare mid 1970's photograph captures the two 'first generation' ships together. The delayed *Norwind* (top) has been joined at Hull by *Norwave* (centre). The ship nearest the camera is *Norcove* on charter to NSF supplementing the former ship's freight capacity. The terminal building (left-centre) was constructed in 1965 and demolished in 1986 to make way for the present three-storey building and customs complex. The ship above the lock-pit entrance is *Baltic Enterprise* of the United Baltic Corporation, at that time operating on the UK/Finland ro-ro services.

(N.S.F. Collection).

Captain Bill Mitchell, master of *Norwave* 1974/87, guides the ship to its Zeebrugge berth from the starboard side bridge wing. (Pictured October 1985).

The bridgehouse *Norwave/Norwind* was a blend of up-to-date navigational aids and traditional woodwork. Sadly the latter is far less obvious in present day ships. The photo highlights *Norwind*'s pristine condition in her last years with N.S.F. (Jan Meyer).

Norwave celebrates the arrival of big sister *Norland* by escorting the new vessel on her first North Sea voyage, June 1974. (N.S.F. Collection).

Sad farewell. Evening sunlight spotlights *Norwind* on 5th July 1987 as she commences her last voyage for N.S.F. and leaves Hull forever. On arrival at Zeebrugge the ship discharged and was taken on a short canal journey to Brugges, where she was laid-up pending collection by her new owners, Ventouris Line, three months later.
(Michael Drewery).

Norland shows her fine lines while speeding to Rotterdam on her maiden voyage, June 1974.
(N.S.F. Collection).

2.   The Second Generation - Norland/Norstar

On her arrival at Hull 10th June 1974 *Norland* was listed as the largest ferry of her kind in the world. Dressed overall and immaculate in the company's then black/white/orange livery the new ship towered above all else, seemingly overreaching anything previously seen at the dock.

Added to the obvious reasons for celebration was the relief of seeing the big ship brought through the infamous lock at King George Dock. Measuring 25.20 metres breadth the 'second generation' vessels had been designed to literally squeeze between the 25.90 metre wide lock walls. Certainly not last to breathe a sigh of relief amongst company officials was Captain Jim Bodden whose precision handling had proved all the calculations correct.

Six months later her sister ship *Norstar* arrived to the same rejoicing. Obviously the wealth of experience gained through eight years of North Sea ferrying with the 'first generation' vessels had been fully employed in arriving at the new ships' design. Generally their external appearance both in size and lines gave every impression of a medium size passenger liner. Gone were the twin exhausts of the smaller ships, instead a single orange funnel crowned the topmost deck. Equally the previous 'bow door' had been dispensed with - the great breadth of the internal car decks allowing vehicles to 'U' turn at the forward end and discharge back through the stern door.

Internally the designers had aimed to retain the same character as the smaller ships, but the vast increase in size was again the most striking feature. Yet, while keeping such favourite venues as the 'Snug Bar' and providing the same styled restaurant facilities, the sheer capacity of the new ships' public rooms inevitably led to a loss of the intimacy previously achieved. On the other hand, with the addition of such features as passenger lifts, couchette cabins, a shopping concourse, quiet lounges and a Continental Lounge with disco and gaming tables there was much in the new ships' favour.

The popularity of the affectionately labelled 'jumbo ships' was immediate. The vast increase in capacity not only proved invaluable in terms of freight handling, but also lent to greater flexibility in passenger accommodation. Tour operators both sides of the North Sea had already recognised the advantages of linking Northern England to the Continent. Now, with many more overnight berths available, their options were considerably extended. Together with the hard-working 'first generation' ships on the Belgian route *Norland* and *Norstar*'s incessant ferrying Hull/Rotterdam built on an already sound reputation of reliability. Many milestones regarding passenger and freight totals were soon passed, a situation leading to the company being known as the most successful North Sea operator.

Almost eight-years on from *Norland*'s maiden voyage and a catalogue of unimpeded crossings behind herself and sister *Norstar*, the former ship was duly requisitioned by the Ministry of Defence to voyage to the South Atlantic as a troopship. Returning to the Hull/Rotterdam service 19th April 1983 *Norland* had been 'off station' exactly twelve months. (See 'Off to War' page 35). A further eleven week period of absence was registered by *Norland* during the summer of 1985. On leaving Rotterdam her master had to take evasive action to avoid a collision with a coaster under the command of an allegedly drunken captain. Damaged by her own stabilizer touching the bottom *Norland* was towed back to port and her passengers put safely ashore. The ship underwent a major engine room refit returning to her normal duties 23rd August.

During the mid 80's, with the building of the 'third generation' vessels imminent, *Norland* and *Norstar* were subjected to a programme of upgrading. Improved passenger facilities included rearrangement of the restaurants, carpeting of all the cabins and a complete restyling of the Continental Lounges that provided for a more intimate atmosphere.

It was, however, in January 1987 that the most significant decision regarding the long term future of *Norland* and *Norstar* was made.

For some time speculation had been mounting in respect of lengthening the two vessels. An extensive survey had revealed the feasibility of cutting the ships vertically into two halves and inserting a new 20.25 metre mid section. Lengthened as such their cargo capacity would be increased by more than 30%. With a view to commencing the two ships on the company's Hull/Zeebrugge service mid summer 1987 the N.S.F. management awarded the contract to the renamed Bremerhaven yard of Seebeckwerft AG where the vessels were built thirteen years earlier.

On being released from the Hull/Rotterdam run with the arrival of the new 'third generation' ships on May 8th and May 12th 1987 respectively *Norland* and *Norstar* were duly dispatched to their W. German birthplace for the seven week operation.

In conjunction with the 'stretching' of the ships a further programme of accommodation restyling was carried out. The original 350 'G' Deck berths in Standard Cabins beneath the main cargo space were dispensed with in favour of freight. To compensate, the extra 'B', 'C' and 'D' Deck area provided by the new mid section was dedicated to additional Special Cabins. More 'B' Deck cabins were gained by the loss of the original after end Antelope/Snug Bar.

Further to the reallocation of passenger space was the restyling of the previous Forward Lounge. Here the 42 reclining seats were resited on the port side and divided completely from the new attractive lounge area. In their new form *Norland* and *Norstar* each accommodated 881 passengers within the main superstructure on three connecting deck levels.

The external appearance of *Norland* and *Norstar* had not been unduly affected by the lengthening, while the new blue/white livery was well applauded. With their increased facilities and capacity the ships commenced service on the Hull/Zeebrugge route early July 1987.

Whilst on her maiden voyage, December 1974, *Norstar* was welcomed at Hull with the same fervour as that for her sistership *Norland* six-months earlier. The company's '1st and 2nd generation' vessels carried the orange and black livery until 1987. The lettering *North Sea Ferries* was added along the ship's hull in 1979.
(N.S.F. Collection).

Technical Data

	M.V. *Norland*	M.V. *Norstar*
Building Yard	A.G. Weser, Bremerhaven, W. Germany	
Completed	June 1974	December 1974
Port of Registry	Hull	Rotterdam

Services

Hull/Rotterdam	June 1974 to April 1982 April 1983 to May 1987 (Requisitioned by M.O.D. April April 1982 to April 1983)	December 1974 to May 1987
Hull/Zeebrugge	1st July 1987 onwards	6th July 1987 onwards

Before Lengthening

Gross Tonnage	12,988	12,988
Deadweight Tonnage	3,800	3,800
Displacement Tonnage	13,787	13,787
Length	153m (502 feet)	153m (502 feet)
Passengers	1,243	1,243
Cargo	Max. 500 cars or 134 x 12m units + 72 cars or any mix	

After Lengthening

Completed	28th June 1987	4th July 1987
Gross Tonnage	15,047 (26,919*)	15,047 (26,919*)
Deadweight Tonnage	approx. 5,000	approx. 5,000
Displacement Tonnage	17,000	17,000
Length	173.25m (568 feet)	173.25m (568 feet)
Breadth	25.2m (83 feet)	25.2m (83 feet)
Draught	6m (19.5 feet)	6m (19.5 feet)
Passengers	881	881
Cargo	Max. 500 cars or 179 x 12m units + 72 cars or any mix	
Engines	Two Stork/Werkspoor type TM410 totalling 18,000 h.p.	
Service Speed	18.5 knots	18.5 knots
Stabilisers	Fin Type	Fin Type
Crew	99	99
Flag	British	Dutch

* See Nautical Terms page 96

Both Zeebrugge and Rotterdam bound ships load commercial vehicles in a busy mid-70s scene at Hull.
(N.S.F. Collection).

An unusual pre-lengthening aspect of *Norland* while berthed at Europoort (Rotterdam). The picture clearly shows the generous amount of deck space afforded by the 'second generation' ships.

Norstar making a handsome subject on the Maasmond outward from Rotterdam in the mid-70s. Structurally identical both inside and out, *Norstar* and *Norland* differ only in one aspect. Following the same practice as instigated with the 'first generation' vessels, *Norstar* is registered at Rotterdam, flies the Dutch flag and is crewed from Holland, while *Norland* is registered at Hull, flies the Red Ensign and has a British crew.
(N.S.F. Collection).

Helmsman at the wheel of *Norstar* as the ship is guided into Hull by Captain Henk Rijnbergen, Spring 1988. *Norland* has the same bridge layout.

Following *Norland*'s 1983 refit the previous 'Snug Bar' was renamed the 'Antelope Bar'. However, when both *Norland* and *Norstar* were lengthened in 1987 this after-end lounge was discontinued in favour of extra cabin space.
(N.S.F. Collection).

The opportunist camera work of Michael Drewery captures *Norland* in an abnormal berthing situation. The incident took place on the 14th May 1980 during a one-day TUC National Strike. Hull's King George Dock lockgates were not being operated that day and thus *Norland* was obliged to use a very temporary riverside terminal - namely the outer east knuckle of the lockwall. This delicate berthing operation had to be carried out as swiftly as possible for the tide would only allow her ramps to be lowered for a maximum of two hours. From then on as the river ebbed the angle of the ramps became too steep to allow any further off-loading. Consequently all the passengers and their cars had to be disembarked in a very limited time.

Intriguing photographs showing the lengthening process of *Norland* and *Norstar* at Seebeckwerft A.G. Bremerhaven, May-June 1987. Having been sliced in two *Norland*'s forward half was floated out of the dock while the new pre-constructed section was floated in. The photograph shows the ship's three segments being manoeuvered into position.

Following the rigours of the above process *Norstar* is seen at an adjacent berth with her new mid-body sandwiched in position for welding. (Seedbeckwerft AG).

Summer morning sunlight reflected against the gleaming white superstructure of *Norstar* as she arrives at Hull following her 1987 'stretching'.
(Michael Drewery).

NORLAND/NORSTAR PASSENGER DECKS

B Deck

MOON-LIGHT DECK

SPECIAL CABINS

'*B Deck*'. 150 Special Cabins, Moonlight Deck.

C Deck

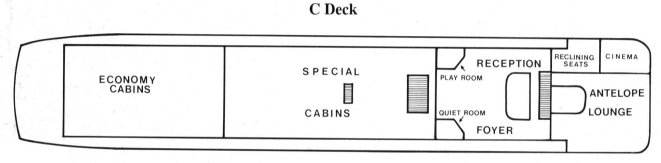

ECONOMY CABINS

SPECIAL CABINS

RECEPTION

RECLINING SEATS

CINEMA

PLAY ROOM

QUIET ROOM

FOYER

ANTELOPE LOUNGE

'*C Deck*'. 67 Special Cabins, 96 Economy Cabins, 42 reclining seats, Reception Foyer, Quiet Room, "Antelope"/Forward Lounge with Bar, Cinema, Children's Playroom.

D Deck

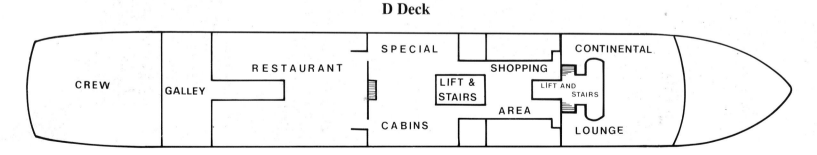

CREW

GALLEY

RESTAURANT

SPECIAL CABINS

SHOPPING

LIFT & STAIRS

AREA

LIFT AND STAIRS

CONTINENTAL LOUNGE

'*D Deck*'. 33 Special Cabins, Duty Free Shop, Perfumery and Gift Shop, Video Games Area, Restaurant with seating for 500, Continental Lounge with seating for 450, Bar, Disco/Dance floor, Gaming Tables.

The sophisticated "Antelope"/Forward Lounge. *Norland/Norstar* underwent major refurbishment in conjunction with ship's lengthening.
(N.S.F. Collection).

The 'D' deck restaurants aboard *Norland/Norstar*, each with seating for 500 passengers.
(N.S.F. Collection).

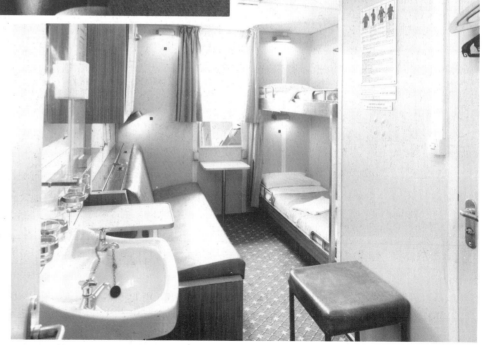

The 217 Special 4 berth cabins aboard *Norland/ Norstar* are located on 'B' and 'C' decks.
(N.S.F. Collection).

Following their 1987 lengthening 'operation', the "second generation" vessels entered the Hull/Zeebrugge service, vastly increasing the company's capacity on that route. Pictured on her first berthing at the Zeebrugge terminal, 29th June 1987, the now 173 metre long *Norland* dwarfs the substantial Leopold II Dam terminal building.
(Luchtfotografie Henderyckx-Izegem).

Having been hurriedly converted to a long-distance troop carrier a heavily laden *Norland* leaves Portsmouth for the initial 8,000 mile Atlantic voyage to the Falkland Islands, April 26th 1982.
The 900 troops aboard from the 2nd Battalion Parachute Regiment line the decks in acknowledgement of a raptourous "send off".
(The News, Portsmouth).

3.

With news of the Argentinian occupation of the Falklands Islands in April 1982, the British Government were obliged to deploy a Royal Navy Task Force to the South Atlantic. Many U.K. registered merchant vessels were requisitioned by the M.O.D. to support the warships in their quest to liberate the islands. Along with a variety of specialised vessels, troopcarriers were a priority requisite. Being at that time the most capacious British registered ferryship, *Norland* was an obvious choice for the long voyage south. Therefore it was more with apprehension than surprise that on April 17th 1982 Mr. Graeme Dunlop, then head of N.S.F., received a notice of requisition.

On the evening of Wednesday April 21st Captain Don Ellerby headed *Norland* down the Humber to the open sea. Unknown to him and the sixty volunteers aboard from her regular crew this was to be the last time *Norland* was to be seen at her home port for $9^1/_2$ months. Having already embarked a contingent of troops at Hull the ship was initially bound for Portsmouth where, after last minute preparations for her new role, she was to complete her loading of 900 personnel from the Paratroop Regiment's 2nd Battalion. An abridged log of her activities under M.O.D. orders reads thus -

April 26th 1982
Norland loaded the 2nd battalion the Parachute Regiment and sailed for the Falkland Islands.
May 7th 1982
Arrival at Ascension Island having called at Freetown in Sierra Leone for fuel and water.
May 7th (evening)
Norland sails to join the Task Force, joining up with the *Canberra,* HMS *Fearless,* HMS *Intrepid,* *Atlantic Conveyor,* *Europic Ferry,* *Stromness* and *Elk,* plus the escorts HMS *Ardent* and *Argonaut.*
May 10th 1982
The convoy proceeded south.
May 16th 1982
They joined the second part of the assault group at an ocean rendezvous. The assault group consisted of *Peerleaf, Plumleaf,*

British Lance, Sir Galahad, Sir Tristrum, Sir Geraint, Sir Percivale, Fort Toronto and the destroyer HMS *Antrim.*
May 18th 1982
The whole fleet met up with Admiral Woodward's *Hermes* Task Force and were poised for the assault.
May 20th 1982
The landing was made at night. HMS *Plymouth* escorted HMS *Intrepid,* HMS *Fearless* and *Norland* followed by *Canberra, Stromness, Europic Ferry* and *Fort Austin* into the Falkland Sound. *Fearless, Intrepid,* and *Norland* anchored close to Chancho Point and disembarked the troops through the shell doors into L.C.U.'s. After the L.C.U.'s had gone the *Norland* weighed anchor and was the first ship to enter San Carlos water, anchoring at Doctor's Point and during the next three hours the whole of the landing fleet entered and anchored. As the sun rose the ship's company found themselves surrounded by the hills of the Falkland Islands. It was the end of their first journey 25 days out of Portsmouth.
May 21st 1982
Norland left San Carlos bay in the evening to rendezvous with *Canberra* at sea. HMS *Ardent* sunk.
May 23rd 1982
Returned to San Carlos Bay. The beach head at San Carlos had had a hard time during these four days with frequent bombing attacks from Sky Hawk and Mirage jets. The Mirages and Sky Hawks pounded the beach head and *Norland* watched almost helplessly as HMS *Antelope* was sunk and other ships were damaged.
May 24th 1982
On this day *Norland* had near misses when two 500 lb. bombs landed alongside her. That night she sailed with the survivors of *Antelope.*
May 25th 1982
Rendezvous with *Canberra* before heading for South Georgia to meet the *Q.E.2.*
May 27th 1982
Norland anchored in Grytviken harbour, South Georgia. In the evening *Q.E.2.* arrived at 2200 and started cross decking the 7th Gurkha Rifles with their equipment plus the 16th Field Ambulance.

May 28th 1982
Norland sailed in the evening for the Falklands and entered San Carlos water again.

June 1st 1982
Landed the Gurkhas.

June 2nd 1982
Loaded 500 prisoners and then sailed to wait offshore with the *Hermes* group.

June 7th 1982
Re-entered San Carlos and loaded another 500 prisoners. Sailed again under the cover of darkness to replenish with fuel and water offshore before heading off for Montevideo to repatriate the prisoners.

June 12th 1982
Norland arrived at Montevideo, discharged the prisoners.

June 13th 1982
Sailed once more for the Falklands.

June 17th 1982
Norland entered San Carlos water for the fifth time and loaded 1,000 prisoners, brought from Fox Bay on *Intrepid*.

June 18th 1982
Sailed from San Carlos to Port Stanley and anchored that evening 53 days and 14,969 miles since sailing from Portsmouth. The night was spent loading another 1,000 prisoners and she sailed the following morning with 2,000 prisoners on board to Puerto Madryn in Argentina.

June 21st 1982
Discharged prisoners in Puerto Madryn.

June 23rd 1982
Arrived back in Port Stanley.

June 24th 1982
Survivors of the 2nd and 3rd Battalions of the Parachute Regiment embarked.

June 25th 1982
Norland sailed for Ascension Island.

July 5th 1982
Arrived in Ascension Island and disembarked the Paras to fly home. *Norland* then loaded the Queen's Own Highlanders plus 15 Falkland Islanders and re-stored for the journey back to the Falklands.

Following the cessation of hostilities around the Falkland Islands *Norland* proved invaluable to the M.O.D. in supporting the garrison established there. For six long months she continuously plied the 3,500 miles between Port Stanley and the Ascension Islands carrying an endless stream of troops and civilians together with thousands of tons of stores and equipment. *Norland*'s crew was systematically relieved by those who had been anxiously waiting on the sidelines back at home.

At the close of 1982 *Norland* and her crew had carried-out a tremendous task, both during the hostilities and throughout the following months of uncertainty in the South Atlantic.

'Falkland Penguin' was the ship's lucky mascot throughout the 66,000 nautical mile voyage. Through pranks and high spirits aboard he sometimes went missing. Happily he was always found in some unusual situation and in the best of health!
(N.S.F. Collection).

But now her orders were for home so, on January 6th 1983 under the command of Capt. Derek Wharton, she weighed anchor at Port Stanley for the final time. By now a familiar sight around the Falkland Islands the N.S.F. ship was given a tremendous farewell by both local people and service personnel. She was escorted to sea by many of the remaining support ships and aircraft stationed there.

At Hull the homecoming was being planned for February 1st, when a huge reception was to be held to honour crew and ship. Having made brief calls at Ascension Island and Las Palmas on the 8,000 mile journey north *Norland* arrived off the East Coast of England on Sunday 30th January. Two days early for the official homecoming and carefully planned celebrations, her master had steered clear of the Humber awaiting orders.

She was initially spotted through the winter mist off Flamborough Head — indeed, being partially camouflaged, rust streaked and weather grimed from the momentous job she had undertaken, *Norland* made an unforgettable sight. By nightfall the ship lay at anchor in the Humber estuary, remaining there until the morning of February 1st.

Plans had been made for sister ship *Norstar*, together with a flotilla of small ships, to rendezvous with the triumphant ferry and escort her homewards along the Humber. Likewise arrangements were made for crew members who had been aboard during the hostilities to be ferried to *Norland* in order to be aboard for the homecoming. However, throughout the night a winter gale had raged. By daybreak the wind was gusting to hurricane force and conditions in the Humber were the worst on record. Not only was *Norstar* unable to meet-up with *Norland* but the proud Falkland's veterans were unable to be reunited with their ship. Together with a rapidly ebbing tide the 90mph wind made the prospect of docking *Norland* impossible so, with much regret, Capt. Wharton had no alternative than head seawards once more.

The elaborately planned reception at the King George Dock Terminal Building, where among 800 guests were civic dignitaries, high ranking personnel from the government and all three services along with the families of the *Norland*'s crew, went ahead on schedule but in the mood of an anti-climax. Back in the river estuary *Norland* rode the storm until early evening when, with a more suitable tide and the wind force down to a mere 'gale', she was finally brought into port. Although the official reception party had long dispersed many hundreds of people gathered in welcome at the quayside. In growing darkness, to the booming of ships' sirens and her shipboard band's rendition of 'Land of Hope and Glory', *Norland* majestically manoeuvred back to No.7 quay, her starting point 9½ months earlier.

In a matter of days *Norland* was to make the short journey down river to Immingham Graving Dock. It was here, over a period of eleven weeks, that she was de-militarised and fully refurbished in a multi-million pound refit.

Completely restored to her former glory *Norland* sailed for Rotterdam once more on the evening of April 19th 1983 - almost one-year to the day from her historic 'call-up'.

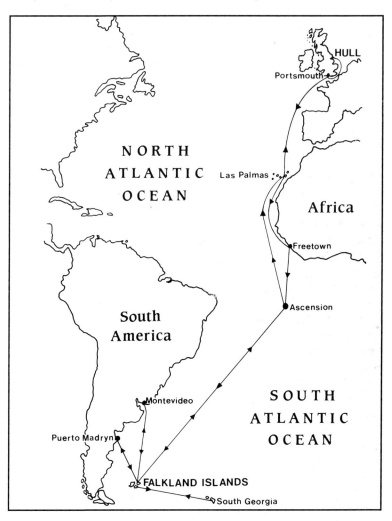

Statistics. While away on 286 days of military service *Norland* sailed 66,093 nautical miles, equivalent to circumnavigating the world three times. In doing so she consumed 10,508 tons of fuel or in shore terms 2,353,948 gallons!
Crew aboard the *Norland* averaged a total of 100 merchant seamen and Royal Navy Personnel.
Passengers carried totalled 13,379 who were fed 571,482 meals.

Norland speeds Southwards to meet-up with the Falkland Task Force.
In order to carry 1,000 men for 60 days at sea the ship had to be considerably modified. The fuel capacity had to be increased to give a range of 32 days steaming. If required she was then able to travel direct from Portsmouth to the Falklands without refuelling. This was achieved by using the ship's ballast tanks which have a capacity of 1,000 tons. These were cleaned and converted to carry fuel oil. Fresh water capacity also had to be increased by loading refrigerated and thirty ordinary containers on the car decks to store food. The ship was fitted with a RAS point (replenishment at sea) to enable her to re-fuel oil and water from the RFA tankers stationed on the route from the U.K. to the Falklands. The ship was fitted with two Sea King helicopter decks one aft and one amidships.
The work was done in Hull and Portsmouth, being completed in nine days.
(N.S.F. Collection).

Target practice for the Paras on the run south.
(Jim Draper).

Norland's crew members "try their hand" over the ship's stern. At this stage of the voyage none of the ship's company was aware that their mandate was to take the ship into the very thick of the hostilities.
(Jim Draper).

Having briefly called at Freetown in Sierra Leone for fuel and water *Norland* arrived at the volcanic Ascension Island after 11 days at sea. Here she joined up with other merchant vessels and a Royal Navy escort.
(Jim Draper).

On approaching the war zone *Norland* becomes a gun ship.
(Jim Draper).

Norland was the first merchant ship to enter San Carlos Water. As the sun rose the ship's company found themselves surrounded by the hills of the Falkland Islands. It was the end of their first journey, 8,173 miles and 25 days out of Portsmouth.
(Jim Draper).

H.M.S. *Antelope* as seen by *Norland*'s crew 23 May 1982. Fortunately the delayed action of the bomb allowed the ship to be evacuated before the explosion. Her survivors were taken aboard the NSF ship.
(Jim Draper).

While in San Carlos Water the Task Force vessels were subjected to frequent bombing attacks. Mirage and Sky Hawk jets pounded the beach head.
Norland stood by helplessly as H.M.S. *Antelope* was sunk and other ships badly damaged.

'Running the Gauntlet' between air attacks, grim *Norland* crew members use a ship's lifeboat to replenish stores.
(Jim Draper).

A Boeing Vertol Chinook helicopter airlifts stores onto *Norland*'s open stern ramp. The Chinook is capable of lifting a huge payload of around 22,000 lbs. They were introduced into the RAF in 1981.
(Jim Draper).

During the course of hostilities 3,000 Argentinian prisoners were embarked aboard *Norland* for repatriation to South America.
(Jim Draper).

While serving as a prison ship the Hull ferry was suitably marked.
(Jim Draper).

At the end of the hostilities the crew found time to relax using the ship's lifeboats for fishing.
(Jim Draper).

While in the role as a South Sea Ferry *Norland* voyaged the 3,500 miles between the Falklands and Ascension Island for six long months. Sports day was a regular event held on the upper helicopter deck en route.

On returning to Government House at Port Stanley Sir Rex and Lady Hunt welcomed *Norland*'s senior officers to the Governor's homecoming party. Second Engineer Jim Draper introduces them to 'Falkland Penguin', *Norland*'s lucky mascot.

Norland battles against hurricane force winds and a strong Humber ebb tide in a vain bid to arrive home for the programmed celebrations. (Hull Daily Mail).

Norland's finest hour. The triumphant ferry arrives home after 286 days of military service, February 1st 1983.
(Michael Drewery).

While *Norland* had been away on active service, replacements for her role on the Hull/Rotterdam route had been sought.

Initially sister ship *Norstar* had worked the passenger commitment on this service alone. By early June 1982 the 5,149 gross tons *Viking 6* had been chartered and retained on the route until late Summer. By that time the more capacious *Saint Patrick II* of the Irish Continental Line had become available. This vessel remained on the Hull/ Rotterdam service until *Norland* returned to her civilian role 19th April 1983.

Neither of these ferries had *Norland*'s passenger or freight capacity. With regard to the latter, supportive ro-ro freighters were chartered to run in tandem with the illustrated vessels. (Michael Drewery).

BUCKINGHAM PALACE

I am delighted to hear that at long last Norland is back from the South Atlantic. Welcome back to your home port.

I, together with everyone in this country, was deeply impressed by the performance of the Merchant Navy in the South Atlantic campaign. I hear nothing but the highest praise for the Officers and Crew of Norland and of the superb contribution you made month after month, often in dangerous, difficult and disagreeable circumstances. I send my warmest congratulations and best wishes to you all.

Charles

Royal acclaim.

Commander Nick Tobin R.N. of the ill-fated H.M.S. *Antelope* salutes *Norland* and her crew as the ship re-enters service on the Hull/ Rotterdam route 19th April 1983.
(Picture courtesy Hull Daily Mail).

4.

House Colours

From its beginnings in 1965 the Company adopted an orange/black cooperative livery together with a compass point house flag/logo.

The ship's hull section was predominantly black rimmed topsides with the marked contrast of white that continued upwards throughout the superstructure. Orange painted funnels and lifeboats embellished the upperstructure, while a broad orange band, running almost the ship's length, was imposed on the black hull. Except for the addition of the lettering *North Sea Ferries* along the hull in 1979 this format remained unchanged until the entirely new two-tone blue livery was introduced in 1987.

This more distinctive livery was first seen on the arrival of *Norsea* from Govan Shipbuilders May 4th 1987. Its introduction was quickly established as sister *Norsun* together with the lengthened *Norland* and *Norstar* took up their new North Sea roles. The departure of *Norwave* and *Norwind* in July of that year saw the last of the original orange/black livery - they were never painted in the new colours.

House flag/livery 1965-87.

Logo/house colours
1987 onwards.

The Dutch flag sister ships *Norstar* (left) and *Norwind* berthed at Hull on the occasion of *Norstar*'s maiden voyage December 1974. The picture gives a clear aspect of the original N.S.F. livery.
(N.S.F. Collection).

Having completed her first commercial voyage out of Zeebrugge, July 7th 1987, *Norstar* displays the new N.S.F. livery against a shimmering Humber ebb tide. During the preceeding six weeks the ship had undergone a spectacular lengthening 'operation' - her new 20.25 metre mid-body is located between the groups of lifeboats.
(Michael Drewery).

This somewhat unusual shot shows the two 6,300 grt. N.S.F. Ipswich/Rotterdam freight service sister shps together at Ipswich. Though not entirely obvious in b/w *Norcape* (left) is pictured in the full present day two-tone blue colours while *Norsky* displays a 'hybrid' livery incorporating the new funnel logo together with the original black and white hull/superstructure scheme. (N.S.F. Collection).

Norland seen in her original black/orange livery for the last time. Under command of Captain Bob Lough the ship was en route Hull-Bremerhaven May 8th 1987 pending 'stretching' at her German shipyard of origin.
(Michael Drewery).

Six weeks later the lengthened *Norland* proudly displays the new house livery on arrival back at her home port.
(Michael Drewery).

Through advantageous wind and tide conditions N.S.F. '2nd and 3rd generation' ships often exceed their normal operational speed of 18.5 knots. This classic photograph captures *Norland* powering the Hull/Zeebrugge route in excess of 20 knots. (N.S.F. Collection).

Showing the N.S.F. colours in a 'brief encounter' are the 'third generation' superferries *Norsea* (left) and *Norsun*. This one-off situation not only captures the unusual event of the sisterships in close company but pictures them in the 'foreign' waters of the River Elbe, Germany. The occasion arose when the ships visited a Hamburg shipyard for their 12 months-guarantee survey, Spring 1988. (Wil Barkmeijer).

5. The Superferries' Arrival - Norsea/Norsun

By the mid 1980's it had become clear that the 'first generation' ships were approaching the end of their operational use for N.S.F. New tonnage was a priority, and orders were subsequently given for the building of two 'superferries'. These 'third generation' ships would have a knock-on effect - by entering service on the Hull/Rotterdam route, they would release *Norland* and *Norstar* which in turn would move to the Hull/Zeebrugge service, replacing the outdated *Norwave* and *Norwind*.

The new 'superferries' were built simultaneously, one at either side of the world. Working for two-years, almost to the same specification, the Scottish and Japanese shipyards were faced with undertones of rivalry as to who could deliver first. A visit to the Clydeside yards of Govan Shipbuilders at the half-way stage of *Norsea*'s building revealed contemporary 'jig-saw' construction methods on what was the first passenger ship to be built there for ten years. Meanwhile, at the Nippon Kokan shipyard, Yokohama, the industrious Japanese with a limited passenger ship building history, waived the need for celebration on launching *Norsun* twelve days in advance of the Govan ship. Consequently the two ships arrived at their home ports within 24 hours of each other - *Norsea* being subjected to teething troubles during sea trials - *Norsun* under the last throes of completion while on her five-week delivery voyage.

In common with N.S.F. practice the company's joint owners had invested equally in the 'third generation' ships - Royal Nedlloyd building the Dutch registered *Norsun* - P&O building the British registered *Norsea*. Apart from then being the largest ferryships ordered for any service from the U.K. the specification was for distinctive cruise style standards of both passenger comfort and facilities. The amenities for up to 1,250 passengers had to include a choice of two lounges and bars, two restaurants, a disco, a cinema, quiet rooms and duty-free supermarket style shopping.

Together with 450 passenger cabins situated at the forward half of the vessels, all the facilities had to be situated on three connecting decks within the main superstructure. These decks were to be identified by an effective colour-code system - Blue, Red and Green. Carpets, curtains, soft furnishings, even cabin key fobs came in subtle colouring appropriate to the deck level. Consequently passengers would immediately recognise their whereabouts from the surrounding decor.

The choice of the vessels' power units was influenced by the need for economy, yet with more than adequate resources to meet the variable North Sea conditions. With four main engines, two nine cylinder and two six cylinder totaling 26,000 h.p., available in any permutation of use, coverage for the strict time-keeping schedules had been well catered for. Two bow thrusters each giving 13 tons of sideways thrust, combined with twin Becker rudders, were chosen to give maximum in-dock manoeuvrability.

On May Day Bank Holiday 1987 a large Hull crowd was confronted with the arrival of *Norsea* new from Govan Shipbuilders. She had finally left the Clyde on Saturday 2nd May completing the 650 mile delivery voyage around the North of Scotland and southwards along the East Coast in 36 hours. Meanwhile *Norsun* was into the final miles of her long-distance delivery voyage from Japan to Holland.

Four days later *Norsea* was at her new Hull Terminal berth. Last minute work had been completed and the ship had been victualled in order to commence her role on the Hull/Rotterdam service. That evening, Friday 8th May, with Captain Don Ellerby in command, *Norsea* commenced her N.S.F. career with all the enthusiasm expected of such an event.

Fourteen hours later, following a convivial on-board party atmosphere throughout the evening across a lake smooth North Sea, the new ship was guided sedately into the Europoort Terminal at Rotterdam to the welcome of a forty-piece marching band. The celebrations at Europoort recommenced on 12th May 1987 when *Norsun* was given an equally rapturous send-off on commencing her maiden voyage.

Engaged in an already esteemed service, *Norsea* and *Norsun* received immediate recognition and approval from the travelling public. In continuing to ply the Hull/Rotterdam route from the above dates the ships have made but minor diversions — on a 48 hour basis Hull/Zeebrugge in releasing *Norland* and *Norstar* for their statutory surveys. Furthermore while gale damaged lock gates were under repair, early in 1990, *Norsun* was diverted from Hull firstly to Immingham and later to N.S.F.'s freight berth at Middlesbrough.

During this period *Norsea* was undergoing annual dry-docking at Rotterdam.

Norsun's Finnish built Wartsila-Sulzer main engines are despatched for the Nippon Kokan shipyard in Japan. *Norsun* and *Norsea* are each powered by two 9ZAL40 nine cylinder diesels (as above), plus two similar six cylinder units. The total output being 26,100 h.p. (N.S.F. Collection).

Norsea/Norsun's Europa Lounge is the centre of the ship's regular night life. Here passengers can dance away the North Sea miles to a resident group. The seating for 300 people is arranged across the entire ship's breadth.
(Studio Acht.).

A stiff westerly breeze tugs at *Norsun*'s overall dress as she arrives in the Humber on her maiden voyage, May 13th 1987. *Norsun* had left her builders at Yokohama in early April carrying 800 Nissan cars to Amsterdam. On discharging she sailed to central Rotterdam for a courtesy visit before entering service out of Europoort on May 12th.
(Michael Drewery).

Norsun/Norsea's funnel weighs-in at over 100 tonnes, it is 70 feet long at its base and rises 60 feet from the topmost deck.
(Michael Drewery).

Technical Data

	M.V. *Norsea*	M.V. *Norsun*
Building Yard	Govan Shipbuilders Glasgow, U.K.	Nippon Kokan K.K. Yokohama, Japan
Completed	May 1987	May 1987
Port of Registry	Hull	Rotterdam
Service		
Hull/Rotterdam	8th May 1987 onwards	12th May 1987 onwards
New Measurement Gross Tonnage*	31,598	31,598
Deadweight Tonnage	6,300	6,300
Displacement Tonnage	19,274	19,274
Length	179m (587 feet)	179m (587 feet)
Breadth	25.36m ($83^1/_2$ feet)	25.36m ($83^1/_2$ feet)
Draught	6.08m (20 feet)	6.08m (20 feet)
Passengers	1250	1250
Cargo	Max. 850 cars or 180 x 12m units or any mix	
Engines	Four Wartsila Sulzer ZA40 (two nine and two six cylinder engines totalling 26,100 h.p.)	
Service Speed	18.5 knots	18.5 knots
Stabilizers	HDW Fin Type	HDW Fin Type
Crew	107	107
Flag	British	Dutch

* See Nautical Terms page 96

Having been named by
H.M. Queen Elizabeth
The Queen Mother,
Norsea slips down the
ways towards the
River Clyde, 9th
September 1986.
The date and time had
been chosen to coin-
cide with the most
favourable tide
conditions to launch
a ship of her size.
(Govan Shipbuilders).

Norsun being prepared for launching at Yokohama, Japan, 29th August 1986. The Japanese do not recognise the launching with a formal ceremony. However, the keel laying is celebrated with a religious ceremony where, from an altar on the slip, a Shinto priest beseeches the gods to bless all those involved in the ship's construction.
(NKK Corporation).

Norsun engaged in sea trials off the Island of Honshu.
(NKK Corporation).

The mist shrouded mountains of the Isle of Arran provide a formidable backdrop for the 31,598 gross tons *Norsea* whilst on her delivery voyage from the Clyde to the Humber.
(Govan Shipbuilders).

A clear blue sky welcomes the sparkling new *Norsea* as she arrives at her home port of Hull, 4th May 1987. The ship had voyaged 650 miles from the yards of Govan Shipbuilders in a little over 36 hours. She made her official maiden voyage on commencing her role on the Hull/Rotterdam service four days later.
(Michael Drewery).

The hi-tech bridgehouse on *Norsea/Norsun* spreads the full 25.36 metre ship's breadth plus the extended bridge wings. The midships console (seen here aboard *Norsea*) is the principal element of three control positions. (Jan Meyer).

The band plays and streamers trail while the tug-firefloat *Lady Susan* salutes *Norsea* on commencing her first commercial voyage. Having entered the River Humber from her King George Dock berth the big ship is being turned 'hard to port' onto the deep-water channel that will carry her the 22 miles to the North Sea. (Michael Drewery).

NORSEA/NORSUN PASSENGER DECKS

Blue Deck

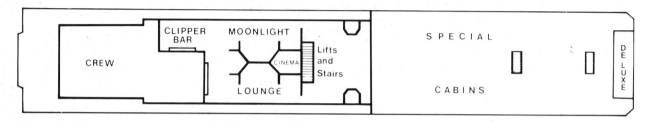

4 Deluxe cabins, 132 special cabins, Cinema accommodating 43 persons, Moonlight Lounge with seating for 277 persons, bar and gaming table, Clipper/Flying Dutchman Bar in aft area.

Red Deck

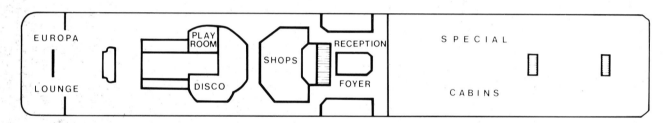

136 Special Cabins (3 for disabled), Reception Foyer and Promenade Area, Duty Free Shop, Boutique and Perfumery, Lighthouse Discotheque, Children's Playroom, Video Games Area. Europa Lounge with seating for 301 persons, dance floor, stage bar and gaming tables.

Green Deck

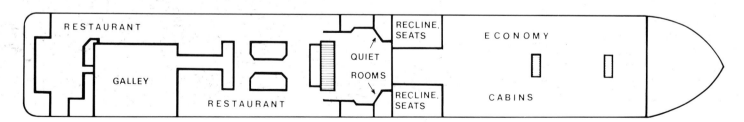

178 Economy Cabins, 131 Reclining Seats, 2 Quiet Rooms (smoking/non smoking), Restaurant with seating for 444 (forward area) and 182 (aft area).

The Moonlight Lounge is situated on *Norsun/Norsea*'s 'Blue Deck'. Since this photograph was taken, its relaxed atmosphere has been further augumented by the introduction of a grand piano, light music being presented as a nightly attraction.
(Studio Acht.).

Much of the passenger cabin accommodation aboard the 'third generation' ships is provided in 'Special Cabins'. They all have en suite facilities and are located on both 'Blue' and 'Red' decks in 2 or 4 berth inside/outside options. All passenger cabins are positioned in the forward half of the ship's superstructure. Being away from the public rooms and distant from engine space, they were sited to offer as quiet a voyage as possible. (NKK Corporation).

The restaurants aboard *Norsea* and *Norsun* are divided into two sections. This aspect of the 444 seat forward section looks aft down the port side. The second section, with 182 covers, continues aft affording views over the ship's stern.
(Jan Meyer).

Norsun in the Pacific, 1987. The new ship speeds from Japan on commencing her 10,000 mile delivery voyage to Holland. During the five-week journey work on the interior was completed.
(NKK Corporation).

6.

An important characteristic of a modern ferry ship is that under all but extreme weather conditions it is equipped to manoeuvre in and out of port without the assistance of tugs. This facility has been arranged by dispensing with the age-old telegraph system between bridge and engine-room. Today's ferry ship captain has direct control over the engines by use of relatively small but highly effective twin levers sited on the main fascia in the bridgehouse and duplicate controls sited at the extremities of each bridge wing. These controls not only govern the power transmitted to the ship's two variable pitch propellers but also decree the amount of pitch to be inclined upon them. For range of pitch and power each lever is calibrated through an arc from zero to ten both ahead and astern.

As varying power is transmitted to the propellers a maelstrom of water is forced onto the vessel's twin rudders set deep under the stern. Consequently the rudders are manipulated advantageously to deflect the ship's stern against this onrush of water.

A further and most essential innovation towards independent handling are the ship's bow thrust propellers. Set in the depths at right angles to the hull these electrically driven twin screws can each operate at up to 13 tonnes thrust either to port or starboard effectually giving the provision of a tug working at the bows.

Using varying permutations of these principal control systems the captain coaxes his ship within restricted confines in a disciplined ritual that constitutes no less than a present day maritime science.

Always there are differing wind speeds and directions that, linked with dockwater turbulance or ever changing river currents, lead to conditions which the ships react to in variable moods. Any wayward tract must be anticipated and immediately detected and countered with the correct application of power. Because of the enormous amount of weight and windage involved unchecked momentum could cause vast damage both to the ship and to shore installations at the waterside.

Backing the master whilst in this process of close navigation is a team of crewmen stationed at strategic points. On the bridge the chief officer carries out the duties of the captain's aide together with handling all the eventualities that arise whilst the master is preoccu-

pied. Here also, at the ship's wheel, an ableseaman answers commands as they are progressively relayed to him. In the engine room, sat before the control section's array of coloured lights, twitching dials, advancing digits and data filled log books are the chief and second engineers. Supported by a p.o. motorman they adjust the ship's mechanical and electrical power systems as instant demands are made on them. On both forward and aft mooring decks, headed by the ship's second officers, are three-man teams of ableseamen; they work on the mooring lines to commands relayed from the bridge. In turn the overseeing officers advise the captain by R.T. of the varying distances between the ship and adjacent quays.

A long-term observer either from ship or shore, standing alongside a captain on the bridge wings or dockmasters at the lockhead, in conditions varying from howling gales to thick fog, from balmy summer evenings to snowstorms on the blackest winter nights, would make no apologies for praising the skills deployed in manoeuvring the N.S.F. ships in and out of the Port of Hull.

To exemplify, once squared with the lockpit entrance either from the tight situation in the dock or from the tidal River Humber *Norland* and *Norstar* at 25.20 metres breadth have only 70cms tolerance between the lock walls over their 173 metre length. *Norsea* and *Norsun* at 25.36 metres breadth have fractionally less elbow room over a running length of 179 metres!

At Hull the N.S.F. captains and their crew have accomplished the summit of shiphandling and earned the respect of all who appreciate the anomalies involved. Their task of docking the superferries at Rotterdam and Zeebrugge is no less formidable. However, the absence of locks and river currents leaves the N.S.F. berths at these ports more readily accessible.

Accepting that every port has its own docking peculiarities and anomalies, it is unlikely there is any other location in the world where ships of comparable size to the North Sea Ferries' superferries are manoeuvered daily within confines that equal those negotiated at Hull's King George Dock. The exercise of coaxing these large vessels from their berth into the main dock basin, turning them centrally in their own length to accurately position and advance through a relatively narrow lock to a tidal river must, unquestionably, be a unique situation.

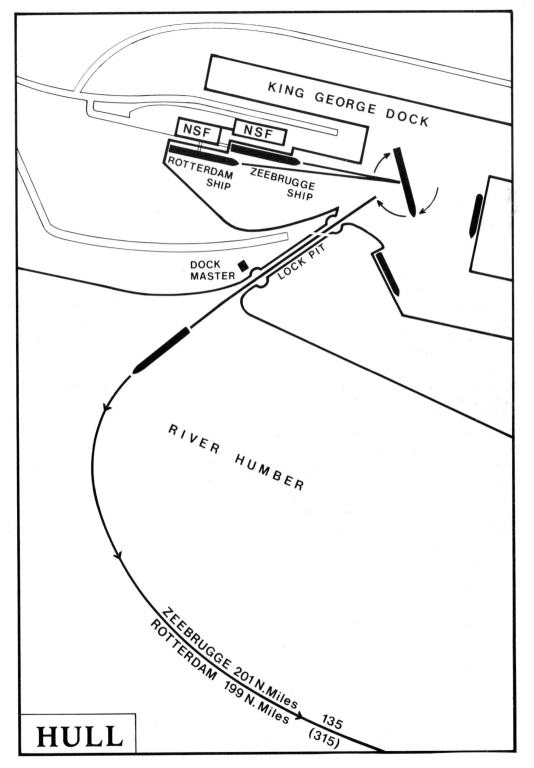

KING GEORGE DOCK

NSF

NSF

ROTTERDAM SHIP

ZEEBRUGGE SHIP

DOCK MASTER

LOCK PIT

RIVER HUMBER

ZEEBRUGGE 201 N.Miles
ROTTERDAM 199 N.Miles
135
(315)

HULL

Captain Bob Lough, *Norsea*, manoeuvres the vessel from its starboard bridge wing - right hand on engine controls, left hand on bow thrust lever. (Since this photograph Captain Lough was appointed to the shore based post of N.S.F. U.K. General Manager).
(N.S.F. Collection).

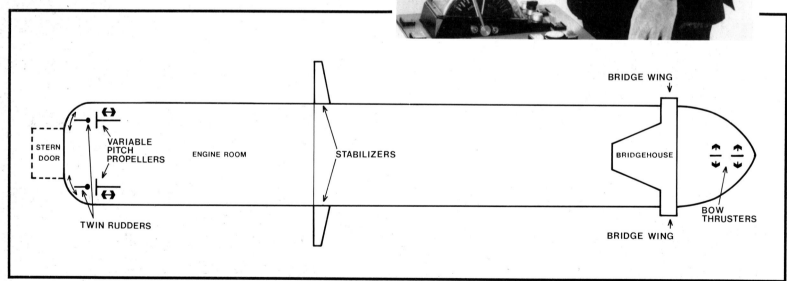

Self Explained principal handling layout (to scale) *Norsun/Norsea*. The stabilisers retract into the ship's hull and are only in the position illustrated whilst the ship is at sea.

Captain's eye view of the lock at Hull as outward bound *Norland* aligns for entry.
(Mike Barnard).

Captain Bert Visser heads the 25.36 metre broad *Norsun* into the jaws of the 25.90 metre wide lockpit.

Norsea encompassed in the lockpit outward bound on her maiden voyage. Note festoons of streamers thrown by celebrating passengers. (N.S.F. Collection).

From the lockside the enormity of the ships is revealed. (N.S.F. Collection).

Port side view looking forward from stern of *Norsea* as she noses out of the lock to the River Humber.

Maiden voyage passengers gaze downwards in awe of the manoeuvre as *Norsea* edges into the lock. May 1987.
(N.S.F. Collection).

7

Since the inauguration of North Sea Ferries on December 17th 1965, the company's advertised schedule has been a daily 6pm departure* from each port at either side of the North Sea to arrive at the destination port at 8am the following morning. This proven long-standing schedule provides a package of a day's driving to arrive at the departure port late afternoon — an inclusive ticket with evening meal, overnight accommodation and breakfast before disembarkation — an 8am arrival facilitating a complete day ahead.

At all three terminals, Hull, Rotterdam and Zeebrugge, foot passenger access to the N.S.F. ships is by covered walkway directly from the terminal building to the vessel's accommodation area. Excepting the arrangement for the Zeebrugge bound ships (*Norland/Norstar*) at Hull the walkways carry passengers straight into the spacious shipboard reception foyer (Zeebrugge bound foot passengers step aboard from the walkway at the after end of 'C' Deck where direction signs lead the way to reception).

Passengers travelling with vehicles drive aboard via the ship's stern door and ramps (present N.S.F. ships do not have bow doors). Lifts and stairways adjacent to the car deck's parking lanes lead upwards to the accommodation area and central reception foyer.

On each vessel all passenger facilities, accommodation and public rooms are located on three connecting deck levels within the ship's main superstructure.

Once aboard ship the passenger is immediately aware of the purser and his staff — their endeavours in catering for the well-being of passengers are seemingly beyond time barriers. On the other hand it is unlikely that whilst underway the passenger will come in contact with the engineering or navigational staff. Much out of the public gaze they too, like the catering department, have a round-the-clock vigil to maintain.

In effect North Sea Ferries' passenger/freight ships are navigated by certificated 'masters' at all times.

Essentially, whilst under close navigation in the Humber and when approaching Zeebrugge or Rotterdam, the captain pilots the ship. He is supported by his watch-keeping chief officer and helmsman. At sea, whilst continually under the command of the captain,

two of the ship's three second officers individually navigate using an auto-pilot and are supported by an able seaman 'lookout'. In the engine room a similar system is operated. Whilst the ship is in close contact with the shore the chief engineer and watch keeping second engineer (supported by a motorman) monitor and adjust the ship's mechanical performance. At sea two of the ship's company of three 'third' engineer officers individually assume watch-keeping duties. The remaining navigating and engineering officers fulfil day-work duties whilst the vessels are in port.

Shipboard Routine

	Bridge	Engine Room
In Constant Command	CAPTAIN	CH. ENGINEER
6 p.m. to 8 p.m.	Ch. Off.	2nd Eng.
8 p.m. to midnight	2nd Off. (a)	3rd Eng. (a)
Midnight to 4 a.m.	2nd Off. (b)	3rd Eng. (b)
4 a.m. to 8 a.m.	Ch. Off.	2nd Eng.
	(supported by	(supported by
	Radio Off. &	P.O. Motorman)
	Helmsman/	
	Lookout)	

In keeping with longstanding schedules the routes on which N.S.F. vessels travel remain equally unchanged. Only exceptional weather or tide conditions divert them from what are long-recognished courses linking Hull - Rotterdam/Zeebrugge. Obviously the time of year determines the amouth of daylight available for an onshore vista during the overnight voyage. However, the following maps describe some of the geographical landmarks and situations notable to passengers on an outward summertime crossing from Hull. The bracketed courses represent the Continent to Hull headings.

* Due to the constraints of the Hull lock system the Zeebrugge and Rotterdam bound ships depart in a space of 25 minutes - the Zeebrugge ferry normally taking priority.

Hull. (The Princess Margaret Terminal).
Built at a cost of £5 million by Associated British Ports for the exclusive use of N.S.F. the present Hull Terminal was put into operation in November 1986. Officially opened by H.R.H. Princess Margaret on July 15th 1987 it stands alongside the site of the now demolished original building. Vast parking areas front the new premises where all amenities for passengers are provided on two floors. The main U.K. offices of N.S.F. are located on the upper floor.

On the River Humber - port side panorama from *Norwind*'s after-deck just one-mile into a summertime Hull-Zeebrugge crossing. The Saltend jetties can be picked-out extreme left.

Aerial view showing the River Humber at high water and (in the lower section) the N.S.F. Hull Terminal complex in 1977. Lying at their No.5 Quay, King George Dock berths, are *Norwind* and *Norland*. Ten years later the terminal building seen adjacent to the ships was demolished. A much larger three-storey building and customs shed was constructed on the site. The vacant quayside astern of *Norland* now serves as the berth for the 'third generation' vessels *Norsea* and *Norsun* operating on the Hull/Rotterdam route.

In the top-centre of the picture the village of Paull nestles near the promontory on the Humber shoreline. Directly below are the Saltend jetties which service the B.P. refinery seen on the left. The empty upper arm of the dock is Queen Elizabeth Dock which was opened by H.M. The Queen in 1969. Central in the picture is the 750' lock-pit linking dock to river. The channel leading from Hull to the North Sea curves from the lock to the top-right corner.

THE HUMBER. Directly after leaving the lock at Hull's King George Dock (see N.S.F. Shiphandling) the ferries are headed seawards down the River Humber at an initial speed of 10 knots. On the port side the Saltend Jetties (1) and their chemical plant backcloth are soon past. Two miles on, having sailed between the Anson and Hebble buoys at an increased speed, the tiny village of Paull broaches the North Bank waterfront (2). Ten miles out of Hull the deep-water channel carries the ship closer to the South Bank. There, to starboard, a marshy unpopulated shoreline (3) gives way to a vast complex of industrial development. Reaching from the shore are the oil tanker and bulk carrier jetties at Killingholme and Immingham which serve the discharge of oil and coal or shiploads of ore for the nearby Scunthorpe steelworks. Hereabouts passengers on the upper decks gain a useful view of Immingham Dock (4) which is linked to the Humber by a lock system similar to that at Hull. Presently Grimsby (5) is abeam — here the 106m (350 feet) hydraulic tower which was built in 1852 to operate the port's lock gates, being the most striking waterfront landmark. Beyond, the renowned northern seaside town of Cleethorpes (6) gradually diminishes with the curvature of the south-bound shoreline. Spurn Point (7) is quickly approached and viewed from the ship's port side. Spurn is a remote place boasting little more than a nature reserve, a disused lighthouse and a small community of seafarers. This comprises of the Humber Pilots' Control Station and, housed in a neat row of cottages set amongst the dunes, the Humber Lifeboat crew and their families. Due to the remoteness and importance of this station the Humber Lifeboat is the only R.N.L.I. craft to have a full-time crew. Over to starboard at this stage, rising gauntly from the depths of the estuary, is the small concrete structure of Bull Fort. Much disused this fortification is an anti-submarine relic of World War I. Within minutes this last outpost is shed astern and, with 23 miles already covered, the North Sea crossing has commenced.

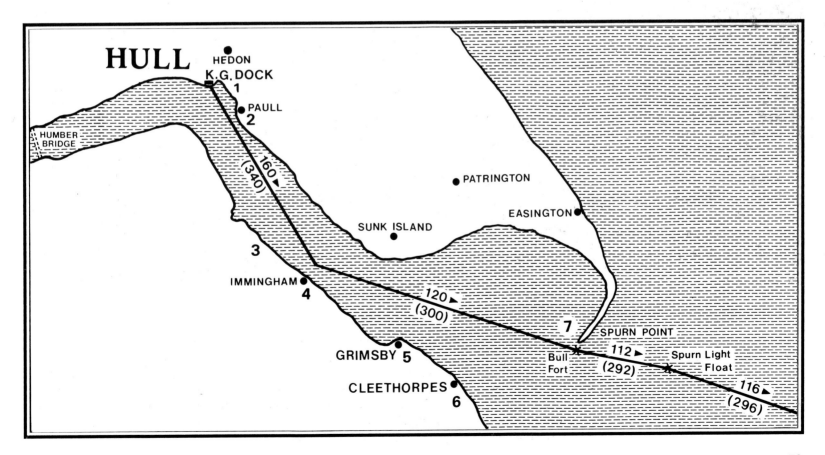

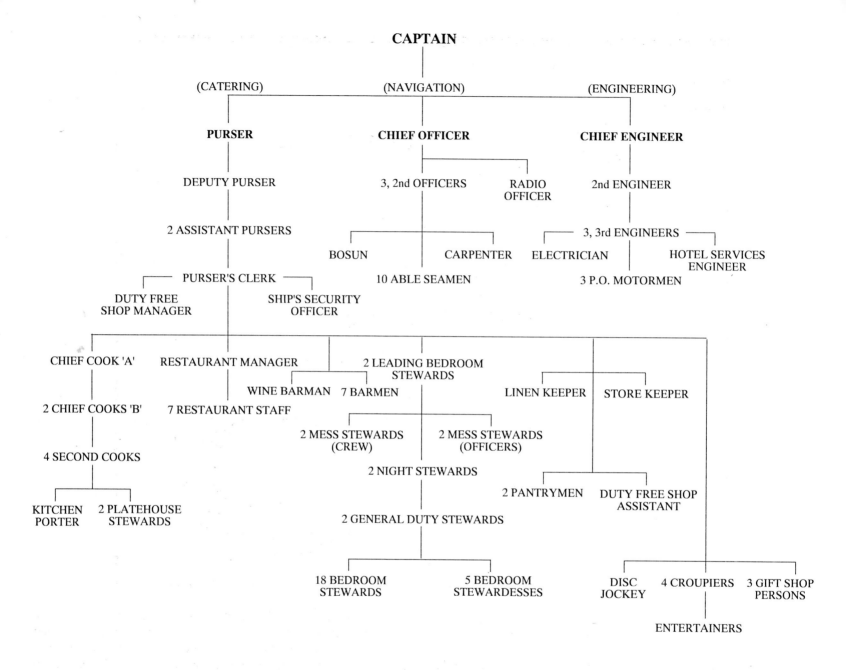

CAPTAIN

(CATERING)   (NAVIGATION)   (ENGINEERING)

PURSER   **CHIEF OFFICER**   **CHIEF ENGINEER**

DEPUTY PURSER   3, 2nd OFFICERS   RADIO OFFICER   2nd ENGINEER

2 ASSISTANT PURSERS   3, 3rd ENGINEERS

BOSUN   CARPENTER   ELECTRICIAN   HOTEL SERVICES ENGINEER

PURSER'S CLERK   10 ABLE SEAMEN   3 P.O. MOTORMEN

DUTY FREE SHOP MANAGER   SHIP'S SECURITY OFFICER

CHIEF COOK 'A'   RESTAURANT MANAGER   2 LEADING BEDROOM STEWARDS   LINEN KEEPER   STORE KEEPER

2 CHIEF COOKS 'B'   WINE BARMAN   7 BARMEN   7 RESTAURANT STAFF

4 SECOND COOKS   2 MESS STEWARDS (CREW)   2 MESS STEWARDS (OFFICERS)   2 PANTRYMEN   DUTY FREE SHOP ASSISTANT

KITCHEN PORTER   2 PLATEHOUSE STEWARDS   2 NIGHT STEWARDS

2 GENERAL DUTY STEWARDS

18 BEDROOM STEWARDS   5 BEDROOM STEWARDESSES   DISC JOCKEY   4 CROUPIERS   3 GIFT SHOP PERSONS

ENTERTAINERS

The tree shows the breakdown of the approximate 100 strong crew of N.S.F.'s '2nd and 3rd generation' vessels. While the captain commands the entire ship's company he is directly responsible for the navigation of the vessel — thus he is positioned at the head of the Navigation Department. The Purser is head of the Catering Departement which, as on all passenger ships, has the most extensive labour force. Forming the third, and equally vital branch of the tree, is the Engineering Department where the 'Chief' is responsible for the function of the ship's entire mechanical systems and ultimately providing its lifeblood — power. There is slight variation in crew complement between the U.K. and Dutch registered N.S.F. ships. Therefore this plan should only be regarded as approximate.

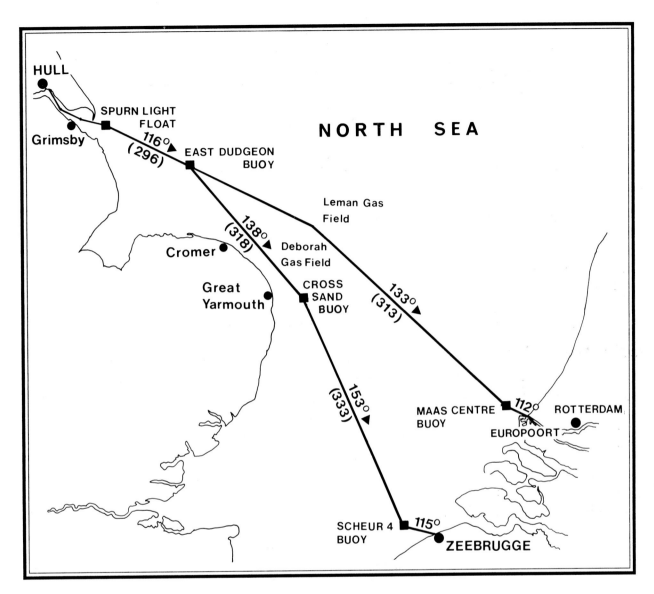

AT SEA. Four nautical miles from Spurn a course of 112 degrees brings the N.S.F. ships to the Spurn Light Float, this being a main exit and entry point for the River Humber. It is now mid evening and here the navigators dismiss the helmsman from the wheel, set the auto-pilot to 116 degrees and enter 'full away' in the ship's log. Now entirely at sea the vessel heads for the continent at 18.5 knots. By 10pm the East Dudgeon Buoy is reached — it is here that the courses for Zeebrugge and Rotterdam separate. Henceforth, until dawn, the only vista is that of lights. From the decks of the Zeebrugge bound ship the twinkling panorama is provided by the distant Norfolk

Coast resorts of Sherringham and Cromer, and later from the Bacton Gas Terminal, Happisburgh and Great Yarmouth. Rotterdam bound passengers see the brilliant and often colourful lights of the platforms of the Leman and Deborah Gas Fields. These well illuminated structures provide excellent static marks for the ship's watchkeeping navigators. Over the after-end rail the normal vista is restricted to the continuous sealane of foaming wake pouring from beneath the ship's stern and into the depths of the North Sea night. Both Zeebrugge and Rotterdam bound ferries are paced to arrive at their respective approach buoys at 6.50 am.

ROTTERDAM. From the Maas Centre Buoy a course of 112 degrees brings the Dutch seaboard within sight. The channel which leads the N.S.F. ship towards Rotterdam's Europoort is maintained at a depth of 22m (72 feet) and capable of carrying some of the world's largest ships. Known as the 'Greatest Port in the World' Rotterdam is a terminal for supertankers, bulk carriers, container and general cargo vessels from all corners of the world. Consequently on approaching or leaving Europoort such tonnage is regularly sited. Guided by 'leading lights' set amidst the wide waterway named 'Maasmond' the ship heads shorewards between (1) a two-mile long breakwater and (2) a similar mole curving round a bight of sanduned reclaimed land. The 17m (56 feet) high dunes are an artificial screen preventing skyline pollution from the huge Maasvlakte oil terminal behind. This terminal provides berthing facilities for vessels of up to 500,000 deadweight tons and is approached from a wide channel (4) viewed from the inbound ferry's starboard side. Dividing the main waterway at this stage is a pencil like separation dam (5). Of the two channels it contrives, the more southerly, named the 'Caland Canal', is taken. Over to port is the channel known as the 'New Waterway' which leads to central Rotterdam and further regions along the Rhine. Seen on its far shore (6) is the Hook of Holland. Although being a small holiday centre the Hook is perhaps better known as terminal for the ferry services out of Harwich. Hereabouts the southern bank (7) displays large up-to-date terminals for the handling and storage of both ore and grain. The N.S.F. ship now turns starboard some 70 degrees and heads sedately along the mile-long Beneluxhaven. On the east bank a further oil installation is passed, but by now the N.S.F. terminal is spotted at the head of this navigable cul-de-sac. Similarly, on the west shore, is the berth used by the cargo ferries out of Felixstowe. While the captain brings his ship's 197 mile voyage to conclusion at the angled mooring dolphins passengers look out at a flat green landscape much of which has been reclaimed from the sea. Europoort is a vast area connecting the continent's sea and road networks, let-alone offering much elbow room to the large petro-chemical industries that abound here.

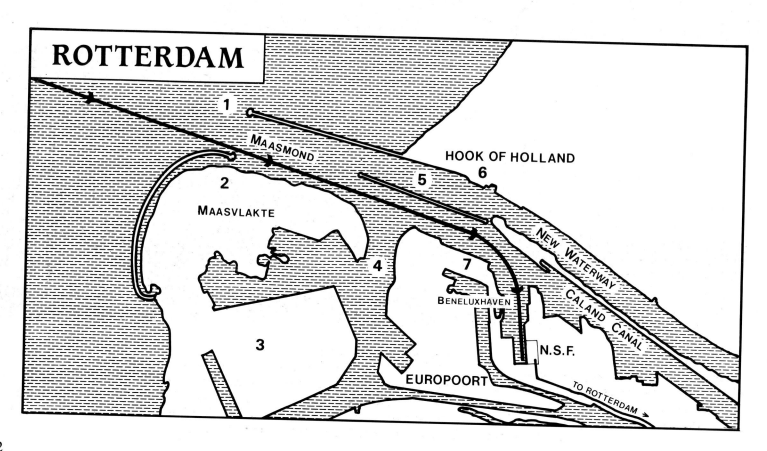

Norsea hides her 179m length in this bow-on photograph taken at the Europoort Terminal. At her starboard quarter is the 3,933 gross tons German registered *Argo* which was chartered to operate on the company's Ipswich/Rotterdam freight route 1986-89, and Hull/Rotterdam as back-up freighter mid-1991 onwards.

Rotterdam. (Europoort).

The upper floors at the Europoort Terminal accommodate N.S.F.'s headquarters. Opened in 1974 in conjunction with the arrival of *Norland* and *Norstar* the building has from then been subjected to a steady programme of updating. In 1990 an entirely new walkway system was constructed. This provided foot passengers with a more leisurely route between ship and shore. The terminal and berthing arrangements supersede a nearby complex that is now used for the company's freight operations. The building's spacious reception floor provides all the usual services expected of a modern terminal facility.

This (1985) morning arrival scene was taken from *Norwave* on approaching the, then, recently opened Zeebrugge Terminal at Leopold II Dam. Two years later a passenger walkway was constructed to allow access from 'C Deck' of the '2nd generation' vessels directly to the upper floor of the building.

In operation since May 1985, the N.S.F. Terminal at Leopold II Dam replaced a less accessible base at Zeebrugge's Inner Harbour. The new complex and Terminal Building, which on three floors provides a vast lounge and cafeteria, Customs and Immigration Offices and N.S.F.'s Belgian Offices, was officially opened by Herman de Croo, the Belgian Minister of Transport and Foreign Trade. It was designed with the 1987 switch of *Norland* and *Norstar* to the Hull/Zeebrugge service in view.

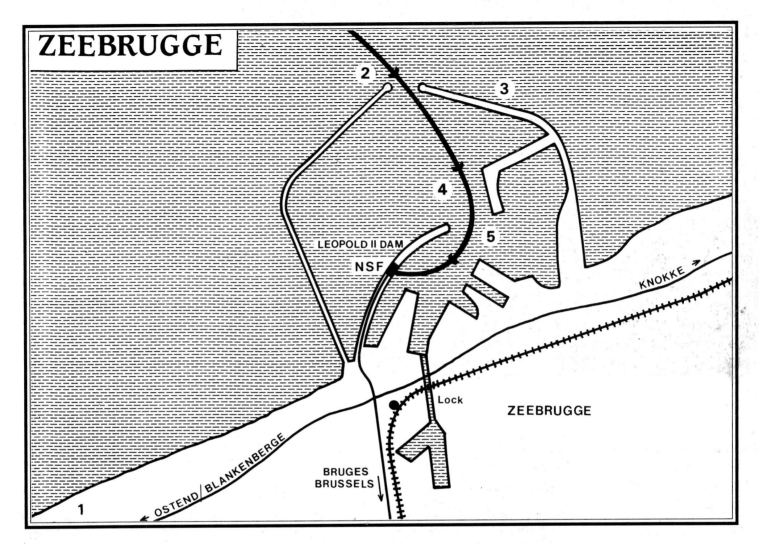

ZEEBRUGGE

Labels on map: **2**, **3**, **4**, **5**, LEOPOLD II DAM, NSF, KNOKKE, Lock, ZEEBRUGGE, BRUGES BRUSSELS, OSTEND/BLANKENBERGE, **1**

ZEEBRUGGE. From the Scheur 4 Buoy a general course of 115 degrees brings the ship within sight of the Belgian coastline (1). At first the shore appears to be flat and featureless but soon, on the starboard side, passengers see a cluster of white painted high-rise buildings. They are at Blankenberge, a fashionable seaside resort some 2½ miles west of Zeebrugge. Soon the wide arms of Zeebrugge's outer mole (2) extend the ship a welcome. Here, on a final course of 130 degrees towards same, one can appreciate the protection these breakwaters offer the port from onshore gales.

Regimentally spaced along the mole walls are numerous modern-day windmills (3) that power generators to supplement the port's power supply. Within the outer mole the ship nears the location of the epic First World War 'Zeebrugge Blockade'. It was here (4) on April 23rd 1918, that British Vice Admiral Sir Roger Keyes had several British ships sunk. This was in order to block the channel used by German submarines based at Zeebrugge. During the Second World War a similar exercise, together with heavy bombardment of the port, was carried out. Zeebrugge was eventually reopened to commercial shipping in 1957 when the last of the blockships was removed. The ship is now slowed and after steering tightly to starboard, enters the Outer Harbour (5) amidst container ships and other ferries. The modern N.S.F. terminal at Leopold II Dam is shortly a prominent feature on the starboard side. The captain brings his ship alongside, manoeuvring the stern hard up to the drive-off ramp. It is 8.30am — the journey completed.

8.

'Freight-Only' Services

IPSWICH/ROTTERDAM (EUROPOORT)

In March 1977 North Sea Ferries commenced a freight-only service between Ipswich and Rotterdam (Europoort). Ironically the chartered vessel used to inaugurate the route, the 5,400 gross tons *Stena Normandica*, was equally a passenger as well as a ro-ro ferry. Regardless, her passenger facilities were sealed off and she fulfilled the role of a freighter with accommodation for 12 transport drivers until delivery of the more purpose built *Norsky* in January 1978.

Of a capacious 9,000 d.w.t. (5,000 gross tons) *Norsky* had been built by Hyundai of Korea under instructions of Sweden's Stena Line and chartered directly to N.S.F. In full company livery she was delivered from the Far East by a N.S.F. crew under the command of Captain Bill Mitchell. On arriving at Ipswich *Norsky* claimed the distinction of being the largest ship ever to enter the port. *Norsky* served the 100 nautical mile Ipswich/Rotterdam route completing one round voyage every 24 hours on a six-day week basis until January 1981. At that time P&O Ferries ro-ro *Ibex* had become available and it was decided to operate her on the service under the name of *Norsea*. Consequently *Norsky* was duly returned to Stena Line.

Measuring 6,300 grt. the former P&O ship has maintained the six day operation since 1981. In common with all ships that have operated on the route she has a service speed of 18.5 knots, full roll on/roll off facilities and accommodation for 12 drivers.

At the Govan launching ceremony of the 'third generation' superferry September 9th 1986, the name *Norsea* was transferred to the new vessel. The Ipswich/Rotterdam *Norsea* then took the name of her predecessor, *Norsky*, and as such continues to ply out of the Suffolk port.

By January 1986 the popularity of the route with hauliers operating between Midlands/South of England and the Continent made it necessary for N.S.F. to increase capacity. Supplementing the service from that date to January 1989 was the 3,933 grt German registered *Argo*.

Following *Argo*'s successful three-year charter *Tipperary* (same class and sister ship to the present *Norsky*) was acquired for the route. Renamed *Norcape* she joined *Norsky* in maintaining the eleven sailings in each direction weekly schedule that commenced in 1986.

TECHNICAL OUTLINE

Norcape (Dutch Flag)	and -	*Norsky* (British Flag)
Service	-	Ipswich/Rotterdam (Europoort)
Tonnage	-	6,310 gross
		3,368 deadweight
Length	-	150 metres
Breadth	-	20.70 metres
Draught	-	5.12 metres
Engines	-	2 x Mitsui, totalling 18,000 h.p.
Speed (Max.)	-	19.4 knots
Passengers	-	12
Freight Space	-	1,450 lane metres

MIDDLESBROUGH/ZEEBRUGGE

March 1988 saw the inauguration of the second N.S.F. 'freight only' service with the charter of the French registered *Aquila*. From the beginning this 1973 built ro-ro proved not entirely suited for the new Northern England/Belgium link. Subsequently, six months later, the 1,597 grt German flag *Wesertal* was brought in to take over the then three round-voyage weekly operation.

As demand on the service gathered impetus a second vessel was chartered. Thus from mid-1989 N.S.F. were able to offer a daily service in each direction, both vessels taking 18 hours on the 275 nautical mile crossing.

Initially the role of the second ship was covered with the charter of the Cypriot flag *Beverdale*. Her charter was for a two-year term concluding summer 1991. This led to *Westeral* being partnered by the *Thomas Wehr* for a short season.

However, it was Autumn 1991 when N.S.F. launched more permanent logistics with regard to tonnage for their Middlesbrough/Zeebrugge service. At this time the 6,850 grt. Finnish flag ro-ro freighters *Bore King* and *Bore Queen* were chartered and brought into service as *Norking* and *Norqueen* with long-term objectives for

this relatively new operation in view. The introduction of these considerably larger ships vastly increased capacity and with their improved service speed of 17.5 knots reduced the crossing schedule to 15 hours.

A large volume of the freight shipped on this route is related to the chemical and allied industries. Labelled as hazardous cargo this is freight prohibited aboard passenger ferries.

A splendid aspect of the 6,300 gross tons *Norcape* leaving Europoort fully loaded on her daily round-voyage Ipswich/Rotterdam service. The 100 nautical mile one-way voyage is run to a $8^{1}/_{2}$ hour schedule (inclusive of river pilotage and docking) with a $3^{1}/_{2}$ hour turn-round time at both ports. The return voyage thus completes the vessel's busy 24 hour cycle.
Norcape entered service with N.S.F. in January 1989 having previously been on long-term charter from parent company P&O to the Irish B&I Line as the *Tipperary*. Like her sister ship and running partner, *Norsky*, which has served on the route since 1981, *Norcape* has a service speed capability of 18.5 knots made available by diesels attaining 18,000 h.p. There is spacious and comfortable accommodation for 12 transport drivers.
(N.S.F. Collection).

Though being a passenger/cargo ferry *Stena Normandica* was the first ship to operate on N.S.F.'s Ipswich/Rotterdam freight-only service. Regardless, the charter vessel's passenger facilities were sealed off and she fulfilled the role of a freighter with accommodation for 12 drivers until delivery of the more purpose-built *Norsky* (the first) in January 1978.
(N.S.F. Collection).

The first *Norsky* operated the Ipswich/Rotterdam service for a three-year period commencing January 1978. This capacious 9,000 d.w.t. vessel is pictured on her delivery voyage from Korea. On arrival at Ipswich she claimed the distinction of being the largest vessel ever to have entered the port.
(N.S.F. Collection).

Seen at Middlesbrough (Teesport) is the N.S.F. chartered German flag *Wesertal*. This 1,597 grt ro-ro vessel gave sterling service in the early days of the Middlesbrough/Zeebrugge operation. She plied the 275 mile crossing for a three-year period commencing September 1988. (Michael Drewery).

The scenic River Orwell forms a twelve-mile passage linking Ipswich and the North Sea. The N.S.F. ro-ro freighters are the largest vessels using the river and are regularly sailing in the company of a variety of wildfowl or all manner of leisure craft in the hands of respectful yachtsmen. This stern-on silhouette of *Norcape* departing from Ipswich characteristics the Orwell scene. (L. Davison).

9. Royal Occasions

H.M. Queen Elizabeth The Queen Mother launches *Norsea* at Govan Shipbuilders, Glasgow, September 9th 1986. The Royal Day marked the first launch and naming ceremony the Queen Mother had performed for North Sea Ferries parent company, P&O, for more than a century. As the Dutchess of York she named the liner *Strathmore* in 1935.
(Govan Shipbuilders).

In October 1974 H.R.H. Princess Margaret was in Hull to open the original Princess Margaret Terminal. On this occasion she was initially welcomed aboard *Norland* by the late Mr. Ian Churcher, long regarded as 'Father of North Sea Ferries'.
(N.S.F. Collection).

H.R.H. Princess Margaret is pictured being hosted on the bridge of *Norsea* by Captain Don Ellerby C.B.E. Her Royal Highness had earlier officially opened the present-day Princess Margaret Terminal, Hull on July 15th, 1987.
(N.S.F. Collection).

(*Above*) Dressed overall *Norstar* celebrates the visit of H.M. The Queen to Hull July 13th, 1977. Her Majesty was aboard the Royal Yacht *Britannia* for a coastal cruise around Britain to commemorate her Silver Jubilee.
(N.S.F. Collection).

(*Left*) En-route from the North of England to a horse driving event in Holland H.R.H. The Duke of Edinburgh (plus Range Rover!) sailed on the August 9th, 1982, Hull-Rotterdam departure. Ironically this was during the period of *Norland's* absence due to her requisition by the M.O.D. The ship to carry the royal guest was the 5,149 ton replacement charter vessel *Viking 6*.
(N.S.F. Collection).

10. Charter Ships (Hull/Rotterdam, Hull/Zeebrugge)

By the early 1970s North Sea Ferries' 'first generation' ships *Norwave* and *Norwind* were at their operational freight limit. Although they appeared capacious at that time the 4,000 gross tons sister vessels were unable to carry all the tonnage available for the Hull/Rotterdam service. Consequently in November 1970 the company added a chartered freight only ro-ro vessel, sailing under the adopted name of *Norcape*, to the route. With a capacity of 47 x 12 metre trailers *Norcape* was in service until April 1972 when the larger *Norcove* was chartered for the run. *Norcove* had space for 60 x 12 metre units and, as demand for freight space continued to grow, she was joined by the similar sized *Norcliff* one year later. These West German registered ro-ro vessels continued to support *Norwave* and *Norwind* until *Norland* and *Norstar* took over the route in 1974. In the meantime *Norcape* had been put to use in establishing the company's Hull/Zeebrugge service on a freight only basis until the arrival of *Norwave* and *Norwind* on the Belgium circuit.

In addition to the ro-ro freight back up between King George Dock and Europoort in the early 1970s was a N.S.F. lift-on lift-off container service operating between Hull's Queen Elizabeth Dock and Prinses Margriet Harbour, Rotterdam. Commenced in 1971 with the cellular container ship *Norbank* on a three round-voyage weekly arrangement, the operation was soon doubled in capacity with the addition of sister ship *Norbrae*. However, through the continuous growth in ro-ro traffic, the company decided to concentrate its activities entirely in that area. Consequently the lift-on lift-off operation was discontinued in 1972.

As the Hull/Zeebrugge service became progressively established *Norwave* and *Norwind* were again operating at their freight limits. Encouraged by the demand from its freight clients N.S.F. chartered the 60 x 12 metre ro-ro *Wuppertal* to supplement cargo space on the route. By 1985 the necessity for a second charter vessel arrived and *Wuppertal* was joined on alternate sailings by sister ship *Fuldetal* (ex *Norcove*).

To continue the charter saga on the Hull/Zeebrugge link two greater capacity ro-ro freighters were introduced. *Thomas Wehr* and *Gabriele Wehr*, each with a space for 91 x 12 metre units, replaced *Wuppertal* and *Fuldetal* during January 1986. From that time they covered nightly crossings in each direction until the lengthened *Norland* and *Norstar* entered service on the Zeebrugge route in the Summer of 1987.

By 1990, such was the demand on freight deck space that N.S.F. were again ready to charter a further cargo ferry, this time to supplement the large capacity *Norsea* and *Norsun*. Thus in Spring of that year the 3,642 gross tons Norwegian registered *Bassro Star* commenced three sailings in each direction per week on the Hull/Rotterdam service to ease space on the two superferries for the ever escalating tourist vehicle trade.

At the conclusion of the Norwegian ship's six-month stint in this 'back up' role the services of the ex Hull/Zeebrugge charter ro-ro *Thomas Wehr* were obtained. Consequently this vessel was back with N.S.F. for a further spell of 9 months, but this time on the 'flag ship' route.

Bringing the Hull/Rotterdam charter ship story up to publication date was the acquisition in mid 1991 of the familiar 3,933 grt *Argo*. This is a vessel much proven through her sterling work on her 1986/89 charter for the Ipswich/Rotterdam service. The long-term future of *Argo* as a charter ship with the company was further endorsed when, in October 1991, she was repainted in full N.S.F. livery and renamed *Norcove*.

Alongside the fore-mentioned principal charters N.S.F. has infrequently acquired ro-ro vessels to cover the absence of the regular ferries during routine surveys, dry docking, maintenance and repairs. The more notable of these 'less permanent' charters were the acquisition of *Viking 6* and *Saint Patrick II* to deputise for *Norland* at the time of her requisition by the M.O.D. 1982/83. To date they have the honour of being the only ships chartered by the company to fulfil a passenger carrying role.

When the transport of dangerous and temperature controlled cargoes was on offer for the Rotterdam route, North Sea Ferries accommodated the situation with the chartered ro-ro vessel *Norcape*. With a capacity of 47 trailers and 80 cars *Norcape* operated a freight only service from November 1970 to April 1972. She was back in service with N.S.F. on November 20 1972 inaugurating the company's Hull/Zeebrugge route. She operated to the Belgian port on a freight-only basis until being joined by *Norwave* in June 1974 and finally being replaced by *Norwind* in December of that year.

During this era, and more recently, charter ships adopted *Nor* prefix names for their term with the company. Presently the name *Norcape* is firmly held by the company's own ro-ro freighter operating on the Ipswich/Rotterdam service.

(N.S.F. Collection).

Seen on completing her first Rotterdam/Hull crossing for North Sea Ferries, March 27th 1990, is the 3,642 gross tons *Bassro Star*. Chartered by the company for a period of six months from that date this 132 metre long Norwegian flag ro-ro vessel exemplifies the size and capacity of the progression of ships acquired to supplement cargo space on the busy passenger/freight routes. A further bonus is that such vessels can carry hazardous cargoes prohibited from the passenger ferries. (Michael Drewery).

Commencing early 1970 was a N.S.F. lift-on/lift-off container service between Hull and Prinses Margriet Harbour, Rotterdam. The route was initially operated by *Norbank* (pictured here). This Liverpool registered vessel was soon joined by sister ship *Norbrae*. This service was shortlived however, being discontinued in favour of ro-ro services the following year.
(N.S.F. Collection).

The 3,933 grt *Argo* is a time-served charter ship with N.S.F. Having spent three years, 1986/89 on the company's Ipswich/Rotterdam service, *Argo* was again on the N.S.F. circuit commencing mid 1991 as back-up freighter to *Norsea* and *Norsun* on the Hull/Rotterdam route. *Argo*'s long-term future with the company was further endorsed when in October 1991 she was repainted in full N.S.F. livery and renamed *Norcove*. As *Argo* she is seen here arriving at Hull at high water August 13th 1991.
(Michael Drewery).

Some Nautical Terms

Port - left hand side of a vessel.
Starboard - right hand side of a vessel.
Bow - the very front of the vessel.
Stern - the back end of a vessel.
Bridge - the control centre of modern mechanised vessels.
Nautical Mile - 1,852 metres (6,080 feet)
Land Mile - 1,609 metres (5,280 feet)
Knot - an international nautical unit of speed which equals 1,852 metres per hour (1 nautical mile).
18.5 Knots - approximately 21 land m.p.h.
Course - the path a ship travels as expressed by the angle subtended between the centreline of the ship and the true north.
Athwartships - from one side of the ship to the other.
Draught - the depth of water a vessel needs in order to float.

Gross Tonnage* - a measurement of a ship's internal volume calculated on the basis of 100 cubic feet = 1 gross ton.
Deadweight Tonnage - the weight in tons of cargo, stores, fuel and ballast a ship is capable of carrying when submerged to her loadline.
Displacement Tonnage - the total weight of the ship and its contents (passengers, cargo, stores, fresh water, fuel etc.). Equally this is the number of tons of water dis placed by a vessel when floating at her load line.

* This long-standing formula has in recent years been subjected to controversial amendments. Subsequently being calculated to revised gross tonnage specifications. *Norsea* and *Norsun* are registered as 31,598 tonnes. Measured accordingly *Norland* and *Norstar* are listed as 26,919 tonnes.

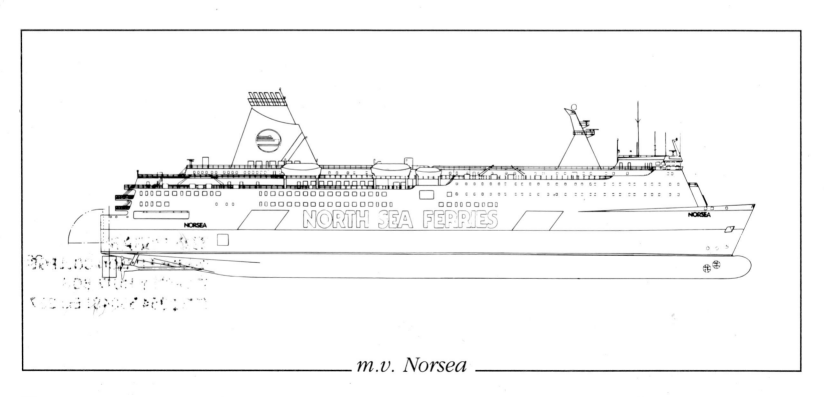

m.v. Norsea